Reference / Career / Business / African-American / Biog

D0837077

The Nation's #1 Book for the Small Black aspiring to obtain Economic Self-Empowerment

You will find information to help you take your small business public. You will find examples of business plans and proposals that will help you in your endeavor to economically empower yourselves and your communities. You will gain economic empowerment.

The story that every African-American should read; the book that every African-American should give to the Small Business Owner, Entrepreneur, Student and Inner City Resident

A complete listing of Investment Institutions, Foundations, Philanthropic Organizations and Government Agencies

▼ The voice of one woman who is destined to economically empower the inner city residents of America.

▼ This book reveals the national plan for Gentrification, the Conspiracy against African-Americans, the real purpose of the Empowerment Zones and the loss of the Inner Cities that were once ours.

▼ The book that everyone who has been displaced by gentrification should read. The book that everyone who desires economic freedom should read.

▼ You will learn Dorothy Pitman Hughes' Lifelong secrets to success and prosperity, and how to build and maintain a thriving business despite the malice of racism, sexism and classism .

▼ You will learn from "A" to "Z" how to fight the system and obtain financing from organizations in the empowerment zones across the United States.

▼ The book that shows you how to write business proposals, business letters, publicity releases, detailed business reports, and who to send them to.

This internationally-acclaimed book has shown thousands of African-American women and men, small business owners and entrepreneurs how to raise money, sell shares, buy stock and get their foot in the door of the billion dollar investment market.

Ms. Hughes, Founder and Organizer of the NYC Agency for Child Development, has owned and operated three day care centers. She is the first African-American woman to own an office supply /copy center and to become a member of the Stationer's Association in the City of New York. She is also the first woman and the first African-American to sell shares in a small business in Harlem. Ms. Hughes is a co-founder of the Agency for Child Development in NYC which cares for 70,000 children. She is a Member of the Harlem Business Alliance, Black Woman Enterprises, The National Black Woman's Political Congress, The National Council of Negro Women, the National Organization of Women, and Women Initiating Self-Empowerment. She is a community activist responsible for changing the lives of thousands of people throughout the world.

This Book will be your constant reference to Economic Opportunities within your Community and Nationally - where to go, what to do, how to get there in the BILLION DOLLAR Public Offering and Stock Investment Industry. It will give you insight to the funding methods used by the Empowerment Zone and tell you how to get what you rightfully deserve. Read the inspiring story of Dorothy Pitman Hughes, who rose from the small town of Lumpkin, Georgia to become one of the loudest voices in Harlem, New York, fighting for the rights of the community. Read her story and learn how to avoid slavery in the twenty-first century by making your small business a success.

US $18.95   CAN $21.95

More Praise for Dorothy Pitman Hughes

"Out of the ashes, there always rises the Phoenix; in the confusion, someone comes with clarity. Meet Dorothy Pitman Hughes, the Queen of Harlem Business."
    —Reverend Al Sharpton, Activist, President & CEO, National
        Action Network

"I'm so grateful to know Dorothy! Nothing is too small or too big for her to take on. She helps me to know that the way of behaving normally is behaving as if everything matters."
    —Gloria Steinem, Founder, Ms. Magazine

"I've always been very proud of Dorothy Pitman Hughes. She is creative and she's wonderful. That which I like most about Dorothy is that she is willing to fight for that which is right; willing to fight for her place in society. Thanks for all the years that you have been struggling; thanks for sticking in there. By fighting for your rights, you've made my rights easier to have access to."
    —The Honorable Percy E. Sutton, Inner City Broadcasting

"Dear Sister, your light is shining in Harlem as a beacon to let others know: the race is not given to the swift, but to him that endureth to the end. We must be willing, as you have been, to apply our energies for our own. Thank you for your inspiration."
    —Hazel Smith, Editor, The New York Beacon

"Ms. Hughes is one of Harlem's resourceful African-American businesswomen who has spent a great part of her life campaigning to build a strong economic base in Harlem..."
    —Kenneth Meeks, Reporter, New York Amsterdam News

"I met Dorothy in the late sixties. The greatest human quality is that of becoming an unstoppable person. She became unstoppable by refusing to quit."
    —Grace Richmond, West Side Community Alliance

"I met Dorothy by way of one of her many passions—stock. her words conveyed the importance of investing in stock, but her heart conveyed the importance of investing in Harlem, our children and our future."
—Vanessa Tyler, Reporter, Channel 11 News

"Hughes is an entrepreneur worried about the exodus of educated young Blacks and the challenge of letting Harlem control its own economic destiny.
—Melissa Lee, Reporter, New York Daily News

"It's been one education working with my mother. Every day I strive to think and be like her."
—Delethia Ridley, Manager, Harlem Office Supply, Inc.

"I have in you, Mom, a constant reminder of what true character and grace are."
—Patrice Pitman Quinn, Film maker, Actress

"There are levels of business that I think all countries around the world should learn from Dorothy Pitman Hughes."
—Reggie Oliver, Business Executive

Dedication

This book is dedicated to my father, Mr. Milton Lee Ridley,
and my mother, Mrs. Lessie B. Ridley.
They gave and gave some more,
so that we could give back.
To my grandson Sean Ridley and all the other children
and grandchildren. They are the future.
And to you, for knowing the future is **now**!

*"As long as there is poverty in the world I can never be rich, even if
I have a billion dollars."*
—The Reverend Martin Luther King, Jr.

Wake Up and Smell the Dollars!

Wake Up and Smell the Dollars!

Whose Inner City is This Anyway!

By   Dorothy Pitman Hughes
        Businesswoman,
        Activist,
        Founder of New York City's Day Care Movement,
        Author of "Alternatives To Welfare" Legislation,
        Mother,
        "Powerhouse".

"Harlem is under siege, as the final phase of a 35 year plan to gentrify Harlem takes effect. The recent designation of Harlem as a Federal Empowerment Zone brings $300 Million government dollars into Harlem under a false banner of economic empowerment for black people; while Disney Corporation and others are poised to take ownership of what black business owners like myself have worked for so many years. Harlem will have transformed from a black community to a white one within the next ten years; and once again, white corporate America and the federal government will reap the benefits of black labor and creativity. It's the nineties contribution to the continuance of slavery into the next millennium."

—Dorothy Pitman Hughes

Wake Up and Smell the Dollars!

Whose Inner-City is This Anyway!

One Woman's Struggle Against Sexism, Classism, Racism, Gentrification and the Empowerment Zone

By Dorothy Pitman Hughes

First Edition
AMBER BOOKS
Los Angeles, CA   Phoenix, AZ

Wake Up and Smell the Dollars!
Whose Inner-City is This Anyway!
One Woman's Struggle Against Sexism, Classism, Racism,
Gentrification and the Empowerment Zone

by Dorothy Pitman Hughes

Published by:
AMBER BOOKS
1334 East Chandler Boulevard, Suite 5-D67, Phoenix, AZ 85048
E-Mail: amberbk@aol.com

Library of Congress Cataloging-In-Publication Data

HUGHES, DOROTHY PITMAN
"Wake Up and Smell the Dollars! Whose Inner-City is This Anyway!": One Woman's Struggle Against Sexism, Classism, Racism, Gentrification, and the Empowerment Zone / by Dorothy Pitman Hughes.
—1st ed.
p. cm.
Includes index.
ISBN 0-9655064-7-9
1. Afro-American business enterprises. 2. Small business — United States. 3. Enterprise zones. 4. Women-owned business enterprises. 5. Hughes, Dorothy Pitman. 6. African-American businesspeople —
Biography. I. Title.
HD2346.U5H84   1999
338.6'422'092—dc21   99-29201
(B)   CIP

10 9 8 7 6 5 4 3 2 1

First Printing April 2000

Contents

Acknowledgments

All praise to God for everything in life.

I humbly thank my children, friends, and customers for standing by me and, themselves, catching the vision to *Economically Empower.*

Delethia Ridley Marvin, Patrice Pitman Quinn, Angela D. Hughes, my grandson Sean Ridley, Paul Quinn, Joan Hamilton, Alice Barnes (Miss B.), Ernestine Ridley, Reggie Oliver, William Pitman, Nicola Licorice, Garfield McIntyre, Vernon Gibson, Doris Gibson, Mildred Dent, Julia Van Matre, Roger Ridley, Alice Ridley, Mary Cunningham, Oscar Walton, Gloria L. Tyrell, Mary Hines, Zo Dodge, Gloria Steinem, The Honorable Percy E. Sutton, Sam Peabody & Family, Ann Miller Boone, Jimmy Booker, Earle Murray, Ohene Darko Iris Bonner Griffin, Hubert Collins, Ms. Lovell, Yvonne Rose, Citra, Valencia, Joan Dawson, Tony Jenkins, Beatrice Smith, Jimmy Mizzell, Susan Taylor, Ed Fordham, George Dwight, Ron Wiggins, Elizabeth "Betty" Harris, Tony Rose, Ron Cooz… and Oprah Winfrey for giving me a much needed vacation.

Special Thanks to:

Zo, Gloria, Iris, Sam, Delethia, Yvonne and Percy.

A Special Acknowledgment:

Tony Rose, Publisher and Editorial Director
Samuel P. Peabody, Associate Publisher
Yvonne Rose and Patrice Pitman Quinn, Editors
Lisa Liddy, Cover and Interior Design
Mike Armstrong, Cover Photographer

As always the Publisher gratefully acknowledges those whose time, patience, help, and advice have contributed to the success of our literary efforts:

Erline Belton; Philip and Anjie Herbert; Felicia Rose and Kate Saylor; Florence Price; Regina Thomas; Elnora Marie Fleetwood-Miles; Yvonne Marie Fleetwood; Lloyd and Lamurel King; Kevin Anthony Fleetwood, Jr.; John and Mildred Seagraves; Kay Bourne; Cassandra Latney; Therese Fleetwood; Jamila White; Wayne Summerlin; Lisa Liddy; Rodney J. McKissic; Alfred Fornay; Carolyn Herbert; Tom "Satch" Sanders; Samuel P. Peabody; Darryl and Lorraine Sanders; Mrs. Muriel Waller; Mack Lee; Terri Simmons, PhD.; Yvonne Rose; the IBBMEC; the Nation's African-American bookstores; our wholesalers and distributors; the black media; and to Dorothy Pitman Hughes, a modern day heroine whose inspiration and courage have inspired this book.

Foreword

In 1983, Ms. Hughes started on her own to develop needed services specifically for Harlem. She planned, opened and organized a "quick copy" business; and for seventeen years, has operated the successful Harlem Office Supply, Inc. She has become one of Harlem's anchors in business, and has the respect of Harlem's giants in business.

More than a decade and a half after Dorothy Pitman Hughes opened her first Harlem Copy Center on 125th Street, she finds herself in a continued effort to empower the people of the Community. Fifteen years ago, she did so by offering jobs to people along with quality goods and a fast and efficient copy service. Today, Dorothy is applying her lifelong experiences with a national campaign to economically empower the inner city communities. She believes that the only way for Harlem to thrive economically is to get both the public and private sectors to invest and re-invest their dollars in local business. In May, 1997 Harlem Office Supply, Inc, for which Dorothy is CEO, began to privately offer shares of stock at $1.00 a share to individuals, corporations, partnerships and non-profit groups, with a particular interest in ownership by children so that they can build a backbone for their future.

It is common knowledge that Black-owned businesses are always the last to reap the benefits of so-called "Community Grant or Loan Programs. Years of dedication, experience and stamina do not count when it comes to offering improvement assistance to small business owners. When this sort of program was recently initiated in Harlem, Dorothy Pitman Hughes was passed over.

So what, if during the last 15 years, she gave jobs to more than 150 people. So what, if during the last 15 years, she offered quality service to local shops, churches, schools and public buildings in her area. So what, if during the last 15 years, she spent her own dollars with local merchants to help keep their businesses open. So what, if during the last 15 years, she was a community leader who fearlessly fought for the rights of the people. With all of her history in Harlem—business owner for 15 years and homeowner for 25 years—Dorothy, along with all of the other Black businesses on 125th Street, was severely overlooked by the Board of the Upper Manhattan Empowerment Zone.

But, Dorothy is a fighter. The documented facts are astounding: During the 1970's, she co-founded a day care center which became the backbone for the Agency for Child Development established in the Human Resources Administration under Mayor John Lindsay, now supplying daily child care for over 70 thousand children and thousands of jobs for community residents. Ms. Hughes organized the first Battered Women's Shelter in New York, categorized as a homeless shelter. Again, her vision and actions provided a much-needed service while also providing employment. She was a member of the "Governor's Task Force On Rape" and "The Governor's Task Force On Human Services." Ms. Hughes organized a Midtown West Side Campaign Office for the Presidential Election of Jimmy Carter. Ms. Hughes has received numerous letters of commendation and awards, including citations from former President Jimmy Carter, the Late Vice President Hubert Humphrey and the late Senator Jacob Javits. She was also honored by Dr. Dorothy Height, President of National Council of Negro Women with a lifetime membership, and presented with the Legacy of Dr. Mary McLeod Bethune award.

Dorothy Pitman Hughes spent three years on the University Circuit as a public speaker. She teamed up on several occasions with other female speakers such as Attorney Florence Kennedy and Gloria Steinem.

Ms Hughes was founder and operator of three day-care centers, and assisted in the founding of a public community workshop school on the West Side of Manhattan. She has been a guest lecturer at Columbia University, and taught a course called "the Dynamics of Change" at the College of New Rochelle. Presently, she does guest lecturing at City College, Manhattan, sharing her experience of being an African-American female entrepreneur in Harlem.

She is a member of several organizations that are giving support particularly to the economic and social development of the inner cities in the country, i.e: The National Black Women's Political Congress, Black Women enterprises (BWE), The Harlem Business Alliance, Inc. (HBA), The National Council of Negro Women, The Economic Committee of The Harlem Empowerment Zone, The DPH Entrepreneur-to-Entrepreneur Marketing Network and the 125th Street B.I.D.

Realizing the problems of racism, sexism and classism faced by our communities, Ms. Hughes has dedicated time toward founding and operating two organizations which support minority business development. In 1992, Dorothy founded DPH Entrepreneur Marketing Network and Women Initiating Self Empowerment which has registered over 500 women in support of issues surrounding Women owned businesses. In 1995, Dorothy won the rights for herself and her family to purchase their birthright town of Lumpkin, Georgia; and later that year, became the first African-American woman to become a member of the 89 year old organization, Stationer's Association of New York (SANY).

Today, Dorothy is still a thriving businesswoman with her office supply store on 125th Street. She is currently in the process of making a public offering for HOS, Inc. Dorothy is a devoted mother of three daughters: Delethia Marvin, Patrice Quinn and Angela Hughes, and devoted grandmother of one—Sean Ridley; and she has initiated a multi-million dollar lawsuit against the Upper Manhattan Empowerment Zone.

Preface

This book is difficult to write because the final results to be derived from the efforts portrayed here are to be long in coming. While I feel that there is much more to be said and done, I consented to write this book to share with you some of what my journey thus far has been about, and to encourage you to make your own journey toward economic empowerment.

It has been quite a task to come as far as I have in business, given the conditions—economically, politically and socially—and just to have survived this long. I have written this book to show that economic empowerment *is* achievable for our people and that, no matter how long it takes and what degree of hardship the struggle for it entails, it *must* be achieved. It is my hope that sharing my story and insights with you will quicken and ease the process for all of us.

Some of the information written here will seem to have a timeless quality. It is a story both old and new for the generations of us who have been, and continue to be left out of the economic mainstream in America—despite the fact that we have often worked doubly hard in our "pursuit of happiness", in our pursuit of "The American dream."

Harlemites have seen our community go from an economically and socially thriving black community to what often looks and feels like a disjointed "black neighborhood" or "ghetto." And yet we citizens continue to work, to make and spend money. New government Empowerment Zone legislation promises a "leg up" to help us build our community economically, and yet more and more black businesses are failing. Our "pursuit" has not waned, our resources remain, yet somehow, these forces are not coming together to benefit us.

From this kaleidoscope, this collage of intrigue, you may begin to understand that Harlem, as a Black community, is on the line. Questions arise: Has there been, and is there a plan to systematically remove African-American businesses from the corridor of 125th Street and connecting adjuncts? Will Harlem, with its beautiful brownstones, become white only neighborhoods?

We've spent our dollars on rent, and the monies never seemed to go to the upkeep of the properties where we live. We've tried to get loans from our local banks (where we deposit our dollars) so that we can become homeowners and do our own upkeep of our neighborhoods; but our money and the interest on it is never available to loan to us. It has been designated for lending and spending elsewhere.

We've tried becoming entrepreneurs, but can't get loans for business because we have no collateral. Now the new Empowerment Zone legislation says that we are eligible for loans and grants if we are of an ethnic background and/or female, and thus begins the long and absurd process of proving that we are in fact non-white and/or female. But once that is proved, it only serves to work against us. New questions arise: "Who do you know?", "Are they in the loop?", "Who is in current control of that loop or group?", "What is the party line?", "Will you front ownership?"

This book is a call to the residents of Harlem and other inner-city communities to wake up and smell the dollars that we are spending to pay for future controls over our lives! Dollars that we are spending to pay for our removal from our neighborhoods! Dollars that we are spending to ensure the miseducation of our children! Dollars that we are spending to build new prisons to incarcerate our children so that others can profit from their demise! *Wake Up and Smell the 500 Billion Dollars* that African-Americans and Latinos spent between 1997 and 1998! (And we own a fraction of the industries our consumerism supports) Let's wake up and smell the dollars that were spent by us collectively on designer sneakers and oversized clothing that make us look and feel *like we just don't care.* Let us wake up, stand up, and use our dollars in a way that reflects how much we do care.

Yes, the Empowerment Zone brings some opportunity. It brings *much* opportunity for people to be small; to continue to behave as if they were enslaved. There *is* a place for you in the government funding scheme if you are willing to profit from your community's destruction. I choose not to go there. I choose to be a voice in inner-city America and Urban Empowerment Zones screaming, day by day: *Wake Up and Smell the Dollars*!

Dorothy Pitman Hughes

Wake Up and Smell the Dollars!

Chapter One
Lumpkin's Lessons

"Don't take without putting something in."

—Lessie Ridley, my mother

I was born the third child of a family of six girls and two boys to Milton Lee "Rayfield" and Lessie Ridley in Charles Junction, a small community in Lumpkin, Georgia. I remember when I was about nine years old, there were two white children around my age who lived across the tracks from us. (We lived in the last house before the railroad tracks that racially divided the junction). These two children were much poorer than we. While our family had some chickens and hogs and a large vegetable garden, they had only what everyone in that area of Georgia had: a pecan tree in the front yard. The children came just about every day to play with my brothers and sisters and me in our yard. Very often they lingered until suppertime, and my mother would feed them.

One Christmas day the children had spent the entire day playing with us when my mother called the family in for Christmas dinner. Those children didn't look like they had any intention of leaving our front yard, so she asked them, "What is your mother cooking for Christmas dinner?" And they answered, pitifully, "Pee-cans." Pecans. So my mother brought the children in for Christmas dinner and then sent them home, happy and well fed.

A little later, she fixed a plate of food for their mother and sent me across the tracks to deliver it. I walked the few hundred yards to her house filled with the spirit of Christmas. When I got to the

When they were known as "Roger and the Ridley Sisters"—the best Gospel and Church singers in Georgia. (Roger Ridley, Mary Cunningham, Julia VanMatre and Dorothy Pitman Hughes)

house, plate in hand, I cheerfully knocked on the front door. "Who's that?" the woman called out. "It's Dorothy Jean," I said, "My momma fixed you a plate of food for Christmas." The ratty bed sheet on her front window was pulled aside, and she peeked out and said flatly, "Bring it 'round back." So I did, my Christian patience wearing thin. I knocked again. "Set it down on the step," she yelled from the other side of the door. So I took a couple steps back off of the porch and I threw the plate as hard as I could against the back door. *I'm sure a couple pieces of ham must have landed on the step!* Upon my return home, I casually told my mother, "Mrs. (so & so) said she'll bring you your plate back next week."

My stubbornness, my will to survive and to make things better—not just for myself, but for all the people around me—started in Charles Junction. It was an industrious town—a mill town—which provided most of the employment for that region of Georgia. Several counties were supported by the work of my community. Even today, the country's baseball bats are made from lumber from Charles Junction.

In 1990 Charles Junction was sold to Mead Paper Company. My family and all the other Black families that were still living there were evicted from the homes they'd built (our families had lived there for over 125 years). It took us seven years, but my sister Julia Van Matre, my cousin Beatrice Smith and I kept the struggle going and worked to impress upon our families and friends that the shutting down of this community in 1990 would be a loss that would be felt for years to come; and that we could not afford this loss. We found help wherever we could, until finally the three of us found ourselves sitting with our wonderful lawyer, Virdia Greer, at a historic closing where we were able to purchase the town back from Mead Paper Co. in 1997. With God's help, we hope to rebuild our community.

I often say I was fortunate to have been raised in a time and place where the "village" raised the children. I remember that if you were at someone's home at mealtime, you ate there. If you needed to be disciplined, wherever you were, there was an adult there to do so. At school, the first grade was in the same large church room with all the other grades, up to the twelfth. This classroom setting taught me many things; how to listen was one thing I learned that I find most helpful in doing what I do today. We would sit quietly and hear other grades' studies being explained. I could choose role models from among the other youth in the room. I could think out strategies on situations presented to older students, form theories, opinions, and discuss them with my classmates.

It was in this setting that my personality was shaped. My spiritual ideas were formed to a wholeness. One side of my family was Baptist, the other Methodist; some were Primitive Baptist (Orthodox), some Missionary Baptist, some AME Methodist. And there were lots of preachers, deacons and mothers of the church. My mother was Assistant Clerk; her oldest sister was the Clerk. My mother's mother was the first Mother of the church that I knew. Then my mother's twin sister was Mother of the church (she passed away recently). There was a lot of church in my life!

Many other people in the town influenced my interest in show business, politics and business. My grandfather, Andrew Ridley, owned his own family business which my father worked in; and together, they owned a trucking company. Additionally, my father wired most of the homes in our community for electricity and was the neighborhood mechanic. My mother was well known as a songstress. She was a composer as well as a wonderful singer, and her wisdom was sought by many. She also made clothes, baked cakes and did laundry for people; and we children had our own work assignments as well. With all the work she did, "Mudea" (Mother Dear) made sure she gave us each the attention we needed.

Mudea would always remind us to think for ourselves—not be led by "anyone and everyone." She would say, whenever appropriate:

▼ Listen and think before you speak.

▼ Look before you leap.

▼ Treat others as you wish to be treated.

▼ Don't take without putting something in.

▼ Stand on your own two feet.

▼ Don't lean on the wall. Learn to stand up, then you can be sure you're on solid ground.

▼ Feed some from a long handled spoon.

▼ Use the insight provided to you by God.

▼ You don't have to have a large ham bone to choke a mad dog; you can use a cup of butter.

▼ Be careful how you treat people on the way up; you may see them on the way down.

▼ Remember, if you don't love yourself, you can't love anyone else.

▼ When trouble seems all around, just stand still, God will fight your battle.

▼ If you are right and righteous, trust God. You will make it.

▼ If one of your brothers or sisters falls from grace, go to them and help them get back on the road. Be there for each other.

Thank you, Mudea, for all your wisdom.

And thank you for understanding when I decided to leave Georgia; after finishing high school at Lumpkin High Industrial School, with little more than a great basketball record and some good singing and dancing experience.

Dorothy Pitman Hughes aka Jean Myers—when she was performing as a "blues singer."

Chapter Two
New York: An Education

"A man who tosses worms in the river isn't
necessarily a friend to the fish."

—*Malcolm X, 1963*

I left home in the summer of 1957, headed for New York and following a dream to become a great night club performer. I had no contacts in that industry, nor with anyone in New York for that matter. But, determined to go out and explore the world, I used the only option available to me to secure a job. I was recruited by an agency in New York to work as a "domestic." I had spent summers singing at Fort Benning (the Army station) and at night clubs in Columbus, Georgia so I just *knew* that on my days off, I could sing in the New York nightclubs.

When I got to New York, I spent a year in Rockville Centre, Long Island, on Bank Street. I worked as a domestic, and sure enough, I soon started singing in nightclubs. I sang at the Celebrity Club in Freeport, Guy Lombardo's Club in Bay Shore and many lounges on the Island as well as clubs in New York City. My stint as a domestic in New York was short; the "biz" was calling. But the career call I would eventually answer, I had no way of knowing at the time.

Reflecting back, I think of my first entrepreneurial experience—making egg sandwiches and selling them to the children at stick ball games on Saturdays—at just eight years old. At ten, I was employed by a neighbor to stay with her mother after I got home from school. While in high school, I worked every Wednesday, earning $3.00 for the day. I spent 75 cents for travel to and from work. I contributed 25 cents to a household fund and the rest went toward my savings for school. That $2.25 became my incentive to own my own business.

After leaving the domestic job on Long Island, I bought a washer and dryer from Sears, gave out flyers on the New York University campus in Greenwich Village and I was in business. I operated my business from home, washing and pressing shirts for students during the day and singing at nightclubs in the evenings.

After becoming a mother, it became increasingly difficult to spend the time needed to accept club engagements, and to find care for my daughter, Delethia, while I was working. So I made the decision to take her to my mom in Georgia. But I soon became too lonesome for her and couldn't continue that pattern of parenthood. I brought her back home and started to look for day care service. I was told by the director of the local day care center I visited to go back home, dress poorly and say that my husband was abusive, and that I needed the care "for the protection of the child."

That day I learned so much about myself. I knew that I would never turn my child over to a system that would ask me to lie and give up my integrity and self-respect in order to receive placement for my child. I refused the service and put my show business career on hold to become a full-time activist and childcare advocate.

Dorothy Pitman advocating a bill for children's rights—campaigning for child care services and children's rights to have a better life.

Chapter Three
West Side Story

*Ms. Hughes' determination to fulfill needs and solve problems
begin in the 1970's. Out of her own need, she founded a day-care
center in a room of her Upper West Side apartment. Eventually
the center became the backbone for the Agency for Child
Development, a large public day-care provider, which she co-founded.*

*This led Ms. Hughes into the role of child advocate. As such,
she joined author and editor Gloria Steinem on a three-year
speaking tour discussing women's and family issues.*

—*Crain's New York Business, September 14, 1991*

During this period, I exposed speakeasies in westside housing,
and welfare hotel exploitation of families and children (closing
some of the hotels down). I organized parents to demonstrate for
real care of children and started a "drop-in" day care center in my
apartment.

The tasks of my new career were daunting, but I was very young,
and very creative. One tactic of many I used to call attention to
the problems in the community was to take the welfare check of a
family who was living in one of the most appalling welfare hotels
in the area. During this period children had fallen to their deaths
down faulty elevator shafts in these buildings. Rat infestation and
lead poisoning from chipping lead paint on the walls was a major
problem. The family's welfare check included a direct payment of
$2,000 to the slum lord. I got a colleague of mine, who could
afford it, to cash the family's check and I used the money to put
the family up in Manhattan's swanky Waldorf Hotel for a month.

Ms. Woofe (former Director of West Side Day Care Alliance), Dorothy's daughter Patrice Pitman Quinn and Dorothy Pitman Hughes (Westside Daycare Alliance Founder) with a daycare student taking a break.

I wanted to make the point that the money *is* there for all of our citizens to live a decent life.

Soon, the day care center grew and moved to the basement of the Endicott Hotel on 80th Street and Columbus Avenue, on Manhattan's West Side. Eventually, I was able to build a new building for the center on West 80th Street; a three story building with a large kitchen, large basement for food and equipment storage as well as laundry and office space, two large play areas on the roof, six large classrooms, a nursery for infants; and the building had a long, yellow plexiglass tube running up the middle of it in which the children played "spaceship." In the 25 years I was in day care, I founded three day care centers (one located in Harlem).

While my youngest daughter, Angela, was in day care, I co-founded a public community workshop school, which my two other daughters, Delethia and Patrice, attended.

My advocacy of the Mayor's Task Force on Early Childhood Development led to the creation of the Agency for Child Development (ACD) which I co-founded in 1970. Established in the Human Resources Administration under Mayor John Lindsay, ACD continues to provide care for over 70,000 children daily and provides thousands of jobs for residents of our communities.

At that time, in the area where I lived and worked—the West Side of Manhattan—urban renewal sought to remove lower income groups, and in particular, Blacks and Latinos. In response, I founded The West Side Community Alliance, to fight for the retention of this population, and to offer methods for significantly raising the standard of living for these persons.

While there were outcries during this time about the number of persons on welfare and about the ensuing huge monetary outlays by government, there was no corresponding thrust to provide vehicles for reduction of the welfare rolls or to secure decent paying jobs and services for people to enable such a reduction. When it comes to *constructive* monetary expenditure, which encourages self-development and independence, the poor are forgotten in deference to the established groups, agencies and businesses who service the needs of higher income people.

Proclamation

WHEREAS: THE CITIZENS OF THE BOROUGH MANHATTAN HOLD IN THE HIGHEST ESTEEM THOSE INDIVIDUALS WHOSE CONTRIBUTION TO THE IMPROVEMENT OF OUR CITY IS NOTABLE; AND

WHEREAS: DOROTHY PITMAN HUGHES, FOUNDER AND PRESIDENT OF THE WEST SIDE COMMUNITY ALLIANCE, INCORPORATED, CAN BE INCLUDED IN THE GROUP OF INDIVIDUALS WHO HAVE MADE OUTSTANDING CONTRIBUTIONS TO THE COMMUNITY; AND

WHEREAS: A POWERFUL, TIRELESS, SPOKESWOMAN FOR THE NEEDS OF THE CHILDREN OF THIS CITY, DOROTHY HUGHES ORGANIZED A BROAD BASED MOVEMENT TO ENSURE THE DELIVERY OF QUALITY COMMUNITY DAY CARE SERVICES; AND

WHEREAS: DOROTHY HUGHES PLAYED A PIVOTAL ROLE IN THE ESTABLISHMENT OF NEW YORK CITY AGENCY FOR CHILD DEVELOPMENT, EXHIBITING A STRONG, RELENTLESS COMMITMENT TO THE PEOPLE OF THIS GREAT CITY; AND

WHEREAS: DOROTHY HUGHES IS THE PERSONIFICATION OF THE BEST LEADER AND ACTIVIST THIS CITY HAS TO OFFER; AND

WHEREAS: ON THE OCCASION OF THE 10TH ANNIVERSARY OF THE HUMAN RESOURCES ADMINISTRATION'S AGENCY FOR CHILD DEVELOPMENT IT IS FITTING THAT WE HONOR DOROTHY HUGHES, A REMARKABLE FORCE IN THE STRUGGLE FOR QUALITY DAY CARE AND A FORCEFUL ADVOCATE OF JUSTICE FOR THE POOR; AND,

NOW THEREFORE: BY THE POWER VESTED IN ME AS PRESIDENT OF THE BOROUGH OF MANHATTAN, I, ANDREW STEIN, DO HEREBY PROCLAIM SUNDAY, AUGUST 1, 1982 TO BE:

"DOROTHY PITMAN HUGHES DAY"

IN THE BOROUGH OF MANHATTAN

IN WITNESS HEREOF I HAVE CAUSED THE SEAL OF THE BOROUGH OF MANHATTAN TO BE AFFIXED THIS 1ST DAY OF AUGUST, 1982

_____

ANDREW STEIN

14

The West Side Community Alliance was instrumental in changing history, and gained national prominence. We received substantial support from several private foundations, including private funding from the research component of John Hay Whitney Foundation, the New York Foundation, the Field Foundation, and the Metropolitan Applied Research Center. In 1972, I and my staff researched, drafted and promoted a bill that would amend the Labor Law. It would authorize non-profit community-based corporations to establish training and job programs as an alternative to welfare.

The bill was introduced in the Assembly by Assemblymen Al Blumenthal and Arthur Eve and in the Senate by Senators Manfred Orenstein and Carl McCall (presently our State Comptroller). It was a bill that gave directions on economically empowering people who had been left out of the economic mainstream in America.

I offer you this synopsis of the Alternative to Welfare Proposal and Legislative Bill:

> *The West Side Community Alliance is a major community-based agency located in the Mid West Side of New York City which has been successful in redirecting funds for day care. The Alliance has been responsible for employing, directly or indirectly, over 800 persons, 80% of whom were either trapped in the welfare system or potential victims of it. The Alliance proposes to conduct research that will lead to the creation of the Alternatives to Welfare Demonstration Project in the Mid West Side and to the restructuring of government legislation regarding welfare and marginally employed persons.*
>
> *The essential problems creating welfare are insufficient jobs, and jobs with low pay and little or no benefits. For Blacks, Puerto Ricans and other minorities,*

discrimination increases extensive sub-employment and forces a high percentage of their population into welfare and the low-income category. Also, lack of supportive service hinders employability and causes dependency on welfare. Those persons on welfare who are either presently employed, potential employables, or those who cannot work are forced to carry a stigma, which pervades all areas of their existence.

Public spending for welfare and low-income persons needs to be revamped in order for people to be employed in permanent, full-time jobs paying decent wages and guaranteeing availability of services enabling employment and adequate living. The Alliance believes that given decent jobs, people will voluntarily work as opposed to being forced into present work situations, which are not jobs at all. [At that time, people in "work programs" picked garbage off the street for very low pay and no benefits]. For those people who cannot work, a form of income should be created which does not carry the present stigma of welfare.

The Alliance proposes the redirection of public funds to consist of two aspects. First, instead of money flowing through successive administrative bureaucracies, thereby siphoning off huge sums of money allocated to the poor, money will flow directly through the community. Second, the method of monetary expenditures will be changed to reflect actual individual and community needs as defined by the community.

In creating and operating alternatives to poverty and discrimination, the Alliance proposes to involve a cross section of the community, representing all races, ages, religions, sexes, physical conditions, income groups, and interested agencies and organizations, along with businesses existing within the community. Our program design will use the more effective, universal, rather than selective approach to community problem solving whereby total community involvement will produce total community growth toward self-sufficiency.

Federal, state and local government and private monies will be directed towards unearthing and redesignating jobs, creating new jobs and developing new businesses and service agencies which will employ community residents. The monies will also be utilized to refer people to supportive services; health care, day care, legal assistance, education, housing, and counseling. Jobs, to which residents are referred, will pay decent wages. The goal of supportive services will be to provide comprehensive, quality services. The same public funds that now stagnate people will be used by the people to service their needs. For those who cannot work and must receive income from public spending, new forms of monetary expenditure will be created to eliminate the stigma of welfare.

THE ASSEMBLY
STATE OF NEW YORK
ALBANY

ALBERT H. BLUMENTHAL
**** ASSEMBLY DISTRICT
DEPUTY MINORITY LEADER

720 COLUMBUS AVENUE
NEW YORK, NEW YORK 10025

COMMITTEE
RULES

I.   Title of Bill
     AN ACT to amend the labor law, in relation to authorizing training and jobs for unskilled persons.

II. Producer's Name:
     ASSEMBLY: Albert H. Blumenthal, multi-sponsor—Arthur Eve
     SENATE: Manfred Ohrenstein

III. Summary of Provisions:
     Amends the Labor Law by adding a new Section 217 to authorize not-for-profit community based corporations to establish training and job programs as an alternative to welfare.

IV. Justification:
     Existing work relief employment programs may put welfare recipients to work, but they do nothing to break the individual's dependence on welfare. Furthermore, most members of society, whether on or off welfare, find it desirable for public assistance recipients to become independent, productive, employed members of their community.

     Programs such as the West Side Community Action alliance in New York City have demonstrated the success of supervised job setting within the community in freeing the unemployed and underemployed from dependence on welfare.

     This legislation would authorize such community based programs to receive money from all sources to demonstrate effective alternatives to our present welfare system.

V.   Fiscal Implications:
     None

VI. Effective Date:
     Immediately (1972)

When this Alternative to Welfare Bill was passed, I was told by the then Senator Carl McCall that it had been assigned to the Vera Institute, then headed by Herb Stirs, who went on to become Deputy Mayor of New York City. The larger section of the research for the bill was a proposal, which was funded by HEW (Health, Education and Welfare) and Ford Foundation, but was not funded to my organization. Dr. Charles Hamilton, a professor at Columbia University and an associate at Metropolitan Applied Research Corporation (MARC), and who funded my project for this research, called me into his office to break the news to me that my years of work had been taken from me. While this pained me, I hoped that the project would help us to break the cycle of poverty and alleviate the problems of racism, sexism, and classism.

Despite the rejection we experienced, The West Side Alliance managed to send more than 2,000 people into the work force during its first year. I am reminded of four West Side Alliance youth who were assigned to work on the famous stone cutting project at the Cathedral of St. John the Divine on West 110th Street and who are still working on that project today, more than 20 years later. The concept and programs created then continue to assist families by placing them into the economic mainstream, affording them a better lifestyle.

I was able to push this bill to passing and bring about new programs and money to the state and city of New York, but because I remained Black and Female, I was not included as a beneficiary of the bill. Furthermore, I was isolated by many of those who benefitted from it and still do. So many young African-Americans who climbed up the "ladder of success" that I helped put into place, once they reached the top, began kicking the ladder down.

During the initial years of the program, and the decade to follow, many public officials, organizations and committees requested my input on programs for the people. To this day, many of those people continue to encourage me and offer support to my business ventures wherever and whenever possible. Here, I share with you some of the requests and gratitudes sent to me:

March 19, 1974

Dear Dorothy:

The Assembly Democratic Task Force of the Social Services Committee would appreciate your coming to Albany, New York as an advisor to the committee. The committee is in the process of formulating Social Services Legislation regarding Work Programs and the Supplemental Security Income program.

The members of the committee are aware that the Social Services Legislation now being discussed is of particular interest to you. Your participation will be greatly appreciated.

Sincerely,

Arthur Eve
Assemblyman—143 A.D., State of New York, Albany

June 4, 1975

Dear Ms. Hughes:

Rita Kardeman in my New York Office has forwarded me a copy of the letter you sent her regarding welfare legislation.

As you know, I am a member of the House Ways and Means Committee. The Public Assistance Subcommittee on which I sit will be studying the issue of welfare reform. My colleagues and I recognize the urgent need for legislation in this area. You can be assured that I will seek community input in this area so that any plan we adopt will adequately reflect the needs of the people most affected by it.

I appreciate receiving your views on this matter and look forward to working with you as the Subcommittee begins its work in this area.

Sincerely,

Charles S. Rangel
Member of Congress

Dorothy Pitman Hughes and Congressman Charles Rangel share a moment at Dorothy's fundraiser for the New York State Democratic Party.

October 8, 1975

Dear Ms. Hughes:

I am writing to thank you for your dedicated service on the Human Services task Force. The Task Force's report is an exemplary effort. I commend you on a job well done.

I hope that I can continue to count on your personal help and advice in the difficult months ahead, as we confront the fiscal problems facing our State and local governments while seeking to minimize the impact of these fiscal pressures on those State citizens who most need assistance.

With warm appreciation for your efforts.

Sincerely,

Hugh L. Carey
Governor, State of New York

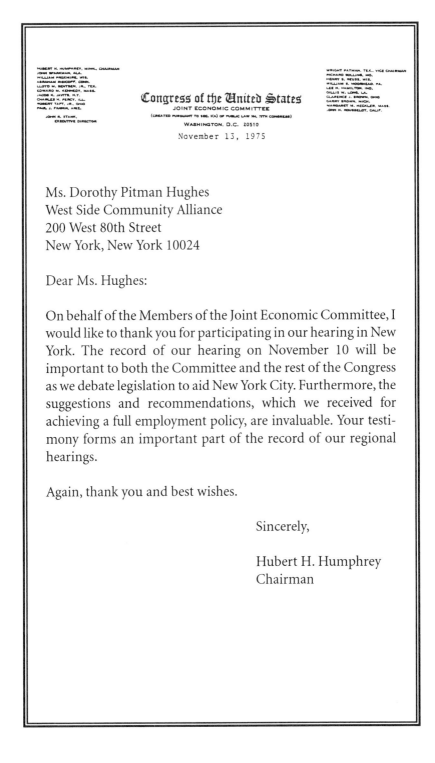

HUBERT H. HUMPHREY, MINN., CHAIRMAN
JOHN SPARKMAN, ALA.
WILLIAM PROXMIRE, WIS.
ABRAHAM RIBICOFF, CONN.
LLOYD M. BENTSEN, JR., TEX.
EDWARD M. KENNEDY, MASS.
JACOB K. JAVITS, N.Y.
CHARLES H. PERCY, ILL.
ROBERT TAFT, JR., OHIO
PAUL J. FANNIN, ARIZ.

JOHN R. STARK,
EXECUTIVE DIRECTOR

WRIGHT PATMAN, TEX., VICE CHAIRMAN
RICHARD BOLLING, MO.
HENRY S. REUSS, WIS.
WILLIAM S. MOORHEAD, PA.
LEE H. HAMILTON, IND.
GILLIS W. LONG, LA.
CLARENCE J. BROWN, OHIO
GARRY BROWN, MICH.
MARGARET M. HECKLER, MASS.
JOHN H. ROUSSELOT, CALIF.

Congress of the United States

JOINT ECONOMIC COMMITTEE

(CREATED PURSUANT TO SEC. 5(a) OF PUBLIC LAW 304, 79TH CONGRESS)

WASHINGTON, D.C. 20510

November 13, 1975

Ms. Dorothy Pitman Hughes
West Side Community Alliance
200 West 80th Street
New York, New York 10024

Dear Ms. Hughes:

On behalf of the Members of the Joint Economic Committee, I would like to thank you for participating in our hearing in New York. The record of our hearing on November 10 will be important to both the Committee and the rest of the Congress as we debate legislation to aid New York City. Furthermore, the suggestions and recommendations, which we received for achieving a full employment policy, are invaluable. Your testimony forms an important part of the record of our regional hearings.

Again, thank you and best wishes.

Sincerely,

Hubert H. Humphrey
Chairman

March 25, 1982

Dr. Eli Ginsberg, Director
Revson Fellows Program
Columbia University
New York, NY 10027

Dear Dr. Ginsberg:

I should like to recommend to you Ms. Dorothy Pitman Hughes, a colleague whom I have known in many different capacities on the Westside of New York City.

Amongst those of us who pretend to deeply care about issues, such as enablement, freedom, power and the like, she is well respected and is an exemplary quality.

I first met Dorothy in the late 50's or early 60's when she was affiliated with Westside CORE. She was the first to address the issue of need for Drop-in Day Care Services, the Welfare Hotel issue, alternatives to welfare, teenage center of rights and responsibilities—the list is endless.

I have had the opportunity to see Dorothy grapple with issues, relate to those who are powerless and interact with policymakers.

She is truly an amazing woman and definitely would be an asset to the Revson Fellows Program.

Sincerely,

Luther W. Seabrook
Community Superintendent
Board of Education, City of New York
Carter Letter

President Jimmy Carter congratulates Dorothy Pitman Hughes at the White House on her successful campaign for child care services in New York City in 1977.

The White House
Washington
May 24, 1977

To Dorothy Hughes

I appreciate your willingness to participate in the Citizen's Review Project of ACTION, and am looking forward to the final report of your findings.

The underlying philosophy of this Project is important and timely. It joins the talents of citizens and nonprofit organizations and from business together with those of government. Moreover, its major purpose is to enhance both the quality of life of communities and the efficiency and effectiveness of government.

I am confident that a new understanding of government and spirit of community will result from cooperative projects such as this.

Sincerely,

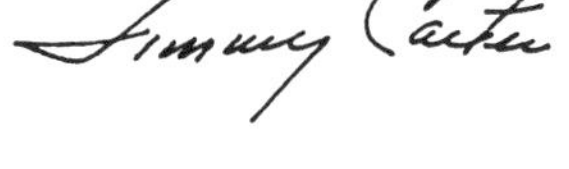

Jimmy Carter

Dorothy Pitman Hughes and other students discussing the future of Harlem.

Chapter Four
Harlem Beckons

What is gentrification?
Webster's says: "Gentrification is the restoration
of deteriorated urban property by middle classes,
often resulting in displacement of lower income people."

While working with the community in the early 1970's, I came across some information that has had a powerful effect on me and the work that I would do for the next thirty years.

I, along with a group of four people from I.S. 201—a public school in Harlem that we were trying to turn into a community school—along with two other community activists from Baltimore, enrolled in a business program at a college in Andover, Massachusetts. The teacher of the course was from Harvard University. After a few days of classes, our group told the teacher that while we were pleased to be learning about other strategies people from other circumstances and with other agendas could use, we wanted to be taught something that was more relevant to our situation. We explained that we wanted to take over I.S. 201 and requested we be taught a course on "power." The teacher refused. We walked out of the class and headed for the campus library. There, one of the brothers from I.S. 201 found an interesting exhibit. In it, there was a 300 page plan for the gentrification of Harlem which would take place over a span of 35 years and culminate in the establishment of Harlem as an entertainment mecca.

Among the strategies it laid out was to strengthen and fund what was then a one-day West Indian parade in Brooklyn; stretching it to a week-long event as part of a move to attract the many West Indians who owned brownstones in Harlem at that time to Brooklyn. Another was to begin to take over Harlem's community-run institutions, starting with Seidenheim and Harlem Hospitals.

Upon my return to New York, I embarked on a mostly unsuccessful campaign to persuade black owners of Harlem brownstones not to sell, and to persuade other black people to buy buildings in Harlem; and I bought a brownstone and moved my family to Harlem.

Dorothy Pitman Hughes and Gloria Steinem when they were on the College and University Speaking Tour.

Chapter Five
Making Harlem My Business

"Helped are those who create anything at all,
for they shall relive the thrill of their own conception
and realize a partnership in the creation of the
Universe that keeps them responsible and cheerful."

—*Alice Walker 1989*

I've learned so much from experiencing ownership in Harlem. *Mostly, I have gained knowledge of how the blueprint for gentrification can be drawn with the participation of the victims. I challenge that if we know how to serve personally, we are obligated to bring others along with us.*

When I speak of Harlem, I tell my story. Your story is probably very similar in your city (especially if it's an inner-city or an Empowerment Zone) anywhere in the United States.

I moved to 138th Street in Harlem in 1972. At this point, I was fully involved in child advocacy and community activism—a role that would continue for the next ten years. During that time, I taught at Columbia University, the College of New Rochelle and City College, and spent three years touring as a speaker with Gloria Steinem, whom I met in 1972 when she interviewed me for New York magazine. We became fast friends and teamed up to speak out on racism, sexism and classism.

By 1982, I had begun to seek other ways to make a living, and I decided on entrepreneurism. I tried to get a small-business loan to start a company. But no bank would risk its money to

Dorothy Pitman Hughes and daughter Delethia building the Harlem Office Supply on 125th Street.

me—black, female, and particularly, with a plan to start a business in Harlem. I was determined to open a fully equipped store providing school supplies, office supplies and office furniture. By offering the same quality, prices and service as midtown stores, I was going to ensure that no one in Harlem had an excuse not to buy their goods within the Harlem community. I paid the mortgage on my home late and used the money to rent a storefront for the first store.

Based on my previous experience, I knew that being a black woman in Harlem wouldn't work to my advantage in opening a business. I knew it would be more difficult to get business loans, establish credit and get top supply vendors to work with me. So, I prepared to open the store without getting credit lines by saving enough money to purchase my inventory through cashier's checks. My foresight was correct. I soon began negotiating contracts with local hospitals and city agencies and going for loans that I never got.

One might say here, that pretty much all one needs to get a loan is a good business plan. But even with a good business plan, containing all the correct subjects and phrases, there are other factors that you must be aware of. Without knowledge of these factors, or if in denial of them, you will not develop the survival techniques needed to maintain and mainstream your business. We have some great role models. These people are featured in magazines each year. As we go beyond the headlines and pictures we realize that they did not get to where they are without a struggle. Black business owners face racism, classism and sexism at every turn. To ignore these factors is to deny yourself the right and the opportunity to entrepreneurship if you are black in America.

Before opening my first store, Harlem Copy, Printing and Stationery Co., in 1983, I researched where Harlem's private and commercial companies spend their dollars. By my estimates, large city and state offices, schools and local residents spend at least $1 million a month outside of the community on office supplies. I thought that if some of that money could be captured within the community to fund jobs and create new businesses, the Harlem community could begin to get on its feet economically.

Seven years later, I moved Harlem Office Supply, Inc. (I had finally reached my goal of having a fully equipped store) just a few blocks from where I had established Harlem Copy—to Harlem's famed 125th street. By then, we employed a total of 17 people—for several of them, removing their dependency upon welfare.

My daughters Delethia, Patrice and Angela supported my efforts and had worked with me in opening Harlem Copy; working with me sometimes seven days a week. Together, we made a decision to draw an active blueprint for economic empowerment. My three daughters assisted me in every phase of the establishment of Harlem Office Supply, Inc. They have engaged in the fiscal day to day, the meetings, and in the folding back of the paycheck in the

Daughter Delethia Ridley Marvin, Former Mayor of Atlanta Andrew Young and Dorothy Pitman Hughes get together at Dorothy's fundraiser for the 1980 Democratic Party Presidential Elections.

interest of the long term goal. But while I endeavored to establish a family business that would support my family and teach my daughters about self-determination and empowerment, my determination to find solutions for the entire community hadn't diminished in my career as an entrepreneur. Although it was a different path from building day care and schools, I was back into my activism role as a community organizer trying to gain economic empowerment for the people.

I formed the *Invest In Harlem Committee.* It served to bring community members together (in my living room at first) to examine ways that local business and industry spent its dollars, and ways to get those dollars to work for Harlem. I began to work, with others, to try to impress upon the people of the community that *we have the means to sponsor our success.*

Reverend Dennis Dillon, a Brooklyn minister who preaches Black Economic Empowerment was of great assistance to me a couple of years ago in bringing this point across to nearly 5000 of Harlem Office Supply, Inc.'s shareholders at a shareholders meeting. He repeated, over and over in his sermons, *"Where we spend our money is where we give our power!"*—a phrase I have adopted, and vowed to repeat as many times as I can.

Where We Spend Our Money Is Where We Give Our Power!

I began to think of how it was when we lived under "Jim Crow" in Georgia. Before integration, we African-Americans owned our own businesses. We ran "total" communities. We bought from each other and we served each other well. We did not cheat each other; rather, we gave more to each other, making sure that every family in our community was taken care of. As white business began to see the benefits of "integration," we allowed what they were *selling*—the idea that they were better equipped to serve us than we—to become part of our mind set. We witnessed the almost complete closing down of our own businesses in all of the states where we had "integration," as we African-Americans moved our spending to white-owned businesses.

Bob Law, WWRL-Radio's "Night Talk" host, points out that it gives us immediate gratification to show whites that we have money, and can spend it on what we want. We began to do a few studies. One showed that on many occasions African-Americans, being ill-treated by white shopkeepers, would bring out the largest bills they had—for instance a one hundred dollar bill to pay for a two dollar item. We will stand outside their stores with picket signs until they let us in on making *their* living! We will become walking billboards for their products—which are often manufactured through near slave labor in this country and elsewhere—with their logos emblazoned across our chests to profit them further.

There are many cultural groups that profit from Harlem's dollars. It has been said that the Business District of the 125th Street corridor from First Avenue to Eleventh Avenue at the Hudson River receives over three hundred billion dollars annually, which goes to take care of thousands of villages outside this country, and does not take care of seven blocks of Harlem. Look around you. Is it the same in your area? Ask yourself, "what can I do? How am I contributing to the continuation of my own economic defeat?"

While trying to establish Harlem Office Supply, Inc. I went to black organizations, churches and businesses; advertising by distributing thousands of flyers to Harlem residents. There are few people in the community who would not know my name or my business. And the fact that I'm still in business is largely because the residents have kept me there. (The business is largely supported by "walk-in" business).

Yet, the *real* dollars that *can* make successful, competitive industries in our communities would be the institutional dollars, spent "on our behalf"; for example, by the public schools in our communities. Check the budgets. Check where the money is being spent. Check the names of the owners of those businesses. Check the name of the person who claims to be in charge. Ask this question: What opportunity will your child have to lead a decent, secure life if the dollars budgeted for their education go to create an economic base in white communities only—creating good, high-paying jobs which put those children in charge of our children's future? And if the person operating the educational institute that is teaching your child and controlling where these budgets are spent is African-American, be aware of the "education" your child is getting.

I went to one African-American district school superintendent who I was sure would understand the concepts of which I am speaking. I selected him because he had been on my staff for three summers at West Side Alliance, while being groomed for his position in the district. Now that he had the job, he did not exercise his power to effect any change in a policy which kept the children under his charge in poverty. He continued, as does the present district administration, to spend their budget outside the community; putting community business in a position where not only do we go unsupported by its institutions, but opportunities we might have had for putting the youth of the district to work—even as delivery people to the schools they attend—go unfulfilled.

I challenged this policy. I went to the Board of Education and bid on jobs for six years. Finally, I started to get an order once a month from the builders of a new school being built in upper Harlem. The monthly order was for one case of toilet paper (of all things), which we delivered to the construction site. I had befriended the young black woman who worked there. One night I received a call from her at home. She told me that I had been "used". She said that I had won the bid for a $58,000 contract, but that it had been pulled and given to someone's son, and used to set him up in business. She said she had been instructed to order a case of toilet paper from me every month in order to get H.O.S., Inc. invoices. I inquired, "Why are you just now telling me this? How could you let this happen?" She said, "I have to take care of my child; and I would have been fired." I asked, "Why are you telling me now?" She responded, "I lost the job."

The fear of losing our jobs has kept many African-Americans giving all of our collective wealth over to others. Some others have found ways to "beat the man" by helping them to use us to do business, with the old, familiar "front game." "You say that it's your business and I'll pay you well. You don't have to do anything but let me use your name."

I didn't get any school contracts. Most churches were still spending their office supply budgets outside the community and many of the major public institutions had set up their own supply businesses. When I tried to get a contract with Harlem Hospital, I was told that I would have to go through Columbia University to get a bid. I learned that Columbia University—whose campus runs from 122nd Street to 110th Street and spans from Riverside Drive to Amsterdam Avenue—had its own office supply company. I'm certain the community doesn't benefit from that spending.

For years I spent money trying to get bids approved. When I bid on printing tests for CUNY, the New York City University System, I could never get the low bid. So I decided to see who was printing the tests for CUNY. I was shocked to find that I was competing with the prison system. Brothers and sisters could not get jobs printing when they were in their communities but now had jobs printing in prison, at a pay rate of between $12 and $15 a week. To add further insult, their prison jobs are blocking their children from getting jobs now—putting them on track to end up in the same place. Prison production is also a large portion of the furniture industry. Our brothers and sisters could have been owning furniture companies, selling office furniture to Harlem Office Supply, had they not been systematically denied ownership. Since then I have learned that prison production is taking over food, clothing and other industries as well. And I'm sure you know the statistics on the disproportionate numbers of our people in prisons.

I am from Georgia. I worked and fought in the movement for civil rights in this country. I know fear. I lived where the KKK roamed and saw family members and neighbors murdered by racism. I have never seen a situation like that of the one in Harlem; where we spend our money against our children's future. We must wake up. We must *Wake Up and Smell the Dollars!*

New York State Department of Economic Development
Division of Minority & Women's Business Development
1515 Broadway
New York, New York 10036   212-827-6266
Fax: 212-827-6293

February 13, 1995
File ID#: 10591

Ms. Dorothy P. Hughes
Harlem Office Supply, Inc.
121 West 125th street
New York, New York 10027

Dear Ms. Hughes:

On behalf of New York State, the Department of Economic Development, Division of Minority and Women's Business Development (D/MWBD) has completed its review of your application for state certification as a Minority/Woman-owned Business Enterprise and has determined that your firm meets eligibility requirements pursuant to Executive Law, Article 15-A.

We are pleased to inform you that the firm of Harlem Office Supply, Inc. has been granted a status as a Minority/Woman-owned Business Enterprise.

Your business will be listed in the State's Directory of certified Businesses with the following list of principal products or services:

Office Supplies (454), Office Supplies and Equipment (459),Office furniture (458), Printing (760), Typesetting (697), Word Processing services (742) and Warehousing and Storing (721)

Certification status is not intended to imply that the State of New York guarantees your company's capability to perform on contracts, nor does it imply that your company is guaranteed any State business.

This certification remains in effect for a period of two years from the date of this letter or until such time as you are selected by this Office for recertification. Please remember that any changes in your company that affect ownership, managerial and/or operational control must be reported to this Office within 30 days of such changes; including changes of company name, business address, telephone numbers, principal products/services, and bonding capacity. At such time as it is necessary for your company to be recertified, you will be notified by this Office.

If your certification status is questioned by any public or private entity, please direct the inquiry to this Office for clarification.

Thank you for your cooperation. On behalf of the State of New York, I wish you luck in your business endeavors, particularly in those involving State agencies.

Sincerely,

Sean Porter
Senior Business Analyst
Business Services Bureau

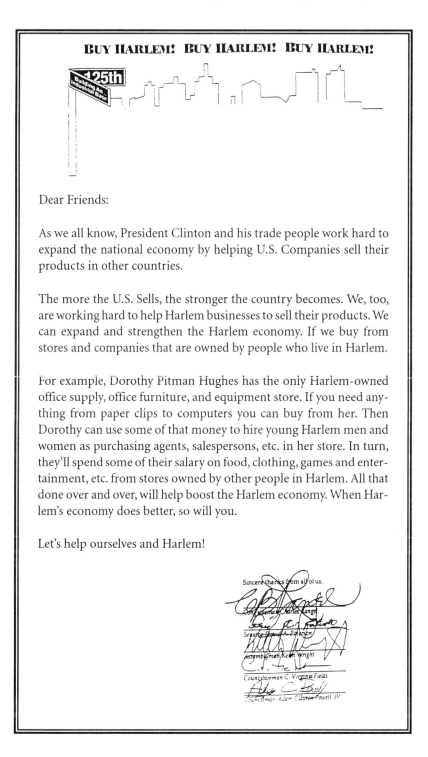

BUY HARLEM! BUY HARLEM! BUY HARLEM!

Dear Friends:

As we all know, President Clinton and his trade people work hard to expand the national economy by helping U.S. Companies sell their products in other countries.

The more the U.S. Sells, the stronger the country becomes. We, too, are working hard to help Harlem businesses to sell their products. We can expand and strengthen the Harlem economy. If we buy from stores and companies that are owned by people who live in Harlem.

For example, Dorothy Pitman Hughes has the only Harlem-owned office supply, office furniture, and equipment store. If you need anything from paper clips to computers you can buy from her. Then Dorothy can use some of that money to hire young Harlem men and women as purchasing agents, salespersons, etc. in her store. In turn, they'll spend some of their salary on food, clothing, games and entertainment, etc. from stores owned by other people in Harlem. All that done over and over, will help boost the Harlem economy. When Harlem's economy does better, so will you.

Let's help ourselves and Harlem!

Sincere thanks from all of us.

Congressman Charles Rangel

Senator David A. Paterson

Assemblyman Keith Wright

Councilwoman C. Virginia Fields

Councilman Adam C. Clayton Powell, IV

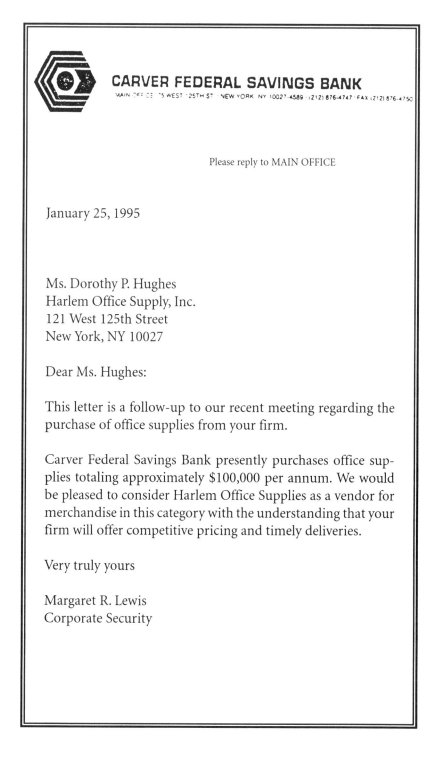

CARVER FEDERAL SAVINGS BANK
MAIN OFFICE 75 WEST 125TH ST · NEW YORK, NY 10027-4589 · (212) 876-4747 · FAX (212) 876-4750

Please reply to MAIN OFFICE

January 25, 1995

Ms. Dorothy P. Hughes
Harlem Office Supply, Inc.
121 West 125th Street
New York, NY 10027

Dear Ms. Hughes:

This letter is a follow-up to our recent meeting regarding the purchase of office supplies from your firm.

Carver Federal Savings Bank presently purchases office supplies totaling approximately $100,000 per annum. We would be pleased to consider Harlem Office Supplies as a vendor for merchandise in this category with the understanding that your firm will offer competitive pricing and timely deliveries.

Very truly yours

Margaret R. Lewis
Corporate Security

*F*ULL SPECTRUM BUILDING & DEVELOPMENT, INC.

275 *Lenox Avenue* • *New York, N.Y. 10027* • *(212)864-7410*
Fax (212)864-7492

February 1, 1995

Ms. Dorothy P. Hughes
Harlem Office Supply, Inc.
121 West 125th Street
New York, NY 10027

Dear Ms. Hughes:

I enjoyed talking to you on Friday about the possibility of Full Spectrum and Harlem Office Supplies working together. As I mentioned at that time, we spend approximately $60,000 or more annually purchasing office supplies, and our needs are growing.

In answer to your question about what our number one priority in doing business with any vendor in this area would be, is that we receive our orders in a timely fashion and prices are competitive with other suppliers in the marketplace.

I look forward to speaking with you again in the near future, and in the meantime, if we can assist you in any way, please give us a call.

Sincerely,

Cynthia Jeffers
Personnel Director

CJ:ds-c

ADAM C. POWELL
Council Member, 8th District

Please Respond To:

☐ DISTRICT OFFICE
198 EAST 116TH STREET
NEW YORK, N.Y. 10029
(212) 427-0700

THE COUNCIL
OF
THE CITY OF NEW YORK
CITY HALL
NEW YORK, N.Y. 10007

March 16, 1995

COMMITTEES:
LAND USE
ECONOMIC DEVELOPMENT
CONTRACTS
STATE AND FEDERAL LEGISLATION
LAND USE SUBCOMMITTEE:
PERMITS, DISPOSITIONS AND
CONCESSIONS

March 16, 1995

Harlem Office Supply, Inc.
121 West 125th Street
New York, NY 10027

RE: Re-purchasing Projections/Commitment

Dear Ms. Hughes:

This letter is a follow-up to your letter dated January 16, 1995, requesting support from our business.

We at Council Member Adam Clayton Powell's office purchase office supplies and equipment totaling approximately $8,000 per annum.

We would be pleased to purchase the amount of $10,000 in office supply and equipment from Harlem Office Supplies, Inc. Providing your firm will offer competitive prices and timely deliveries.

Sincerely,

Frederico Colon
Chief of Staff

44

Chapter Six
Enter the Empowerment Zone

Harlem builds on its tradition of being the Black capital of the U.S. and once had visions of developing international trade between and among "third world" countries through its Trade Center. Black-owned businesses in Harlem had hoped that we would finally be able to mainstream our businesses into the larger American economy. After that endeavor was stalled, we began working to have Harlem designated a Federal Empowerment Zone (EZ). The EZ was a new and exciting government program which would fund economically depressed communities. Funds were designated for people who had been systematically left out of the mainstream economy, and would be allocated over a ten year period in which these communities would demonstrate their economic viability. The Empowerment Zone promised to be our new avenue for building economic parity for our community. Instead, it is putting us out of business.

I had organized the DPH Marketing Network in 1987. Its goal was to develop a support system and information base for African-American entrepreneurs. As the Network grew and communications among business owners increased on the local level, a very bleak reality began to show itself. The sexism, classism and racism that had always worked against us had reached such proportions that most black-owned establishments were on the brink of closing down.

Dorothy Pitman Hughes attends the Black Caucus Meeting in Albany, New York with State Comptroller Carl McCall.

We began to organize a small group of these business owners in hopes of obtaining Empowerment Zone funding to help the owners stay in business. More and more business owners sought to join this group every day. Out of this group WISE (Women Initiating Self-Empowerment) was born.

Getting "Wise"

African-American women owned approximately one third of the businesses in Harlem. Statistics show that minority women never receive more than 0-2% of all state, city and federal contracts and funding. Therefore, if the interest of the Empowerment Zone was to economically empower the people who have been systematically left out of the economic mainstream, there would have been a specific set-aside or allocation of one-third, or 33.3 Million dollars of the funding for the expansion and improvement of the existing female owned businesses in the Upper Manhattan Empowerment Zone; as well as for the development of new commercial enterprises to be headed by women.

Women provided jobs for hundreds of community residents, while addressing employment issues unique to this area. We were, and still are a major source of first time employment for community youth, for which we must also bear the expense of job skills training that our educational system leaves lacking. Collectively, we African-American businesswomen have generated millions of dollars in revenue for this community every year.

Urban Empowerment Zones & Enterprise Communities

U.S. Department of Housing and Urban Development

Empowerment Zone (EZ)

- ▼ Georgia: Atlanta
- ▼ Illinois: Chicago
- ▼ Maryland: Baltimore
- ▼ New York: New York, Bronx County
- ▼ Pennsylvania: Philadelphia/Camden, NJ

Supplemental Empowerment Zone (SEZ)

▼ California: Los Angeles City & County
▼ Ohio: Cleveland

Enhanced Enterprise Community (EEC)

▼ California: Oakland
▼ Massachusetts: Boston
▼ Missouri: Kansas city (MO) and (KS)
▼ Texas: Houston

Enterprise Community

▼ Alabama: Birmingham
▼ Arizona: Phoenix
▼ Arkansas: Pulaski County/Little Rock
▼ California: Los Angeles/Huntington Park
▼ California: San Diego
▼ California: San Francisco/Bayview/Hunters Point
▼ Colorado: Denver
▼ Connecticut: Bridgeport
▼ Connecticut: New Haven
▼ Delaware: Wilmington
▼ District of Columbia: Washington
▼ Florida: Dade County, Miami
▼ Georgia: Albany
▼ Illinois: East St. Louis, Springfield
▼ Indiana: Indianapolis
▼ Iowa: Des Moines
▼ Kentucky: Louisville
▼ Louisiana: New Orleans, Ouachita Parish
▼ Massachusetts: Lowell, Springfield
▼ Michigan: Flint, Muskegon
▼ Minnesota: Minneapolis, St. Paul
▼ Mississippi: Jackson
▼ Missouri: St. Louis

- ▼ Nebraska: Omaha
- ▼ Nevada: Clark County/Las Vegas
- ▼ New Hampshire: Manchester
- ▼ New Jersey: Newark
- ▼ New Mexico: Albuquerque
- ▼ New York: Albany, Buffalo, Newburgh/Kingston, Rochester, Schenectady, Troy
- ▼ North Carolina: Charlotte
- ▼ Ohio: Akron, Columbus
- ▼ Oklahoma: Oklahoma City
- ▼ Oregon: Portland
- ▼ Pennsylvania: Harrisburg, Pittsburgh
- ▼ Rhode Island: Providence
- ▼ South Carolina: Charleston
- ▼ Tennessee: Memphis, Nashville
- ▼ Texas: Dallas, El Paso, San Antonio, Waco
- ▼ Utah: Ogden
- ▼ Vermont: Burlington
- ▼ Virginia: Norfolk
- ▼ Washington: Seattle, Tacoma
- ▼ West Virginia: Huntington
- ▼ Wisconsin: Milwaukee

The African-American vision of ourselves in Harlem's empowerment plan was one in which our entrepreneurial achievements and endeavors would finally be given the respect they command. Each and every business owner in this community was ready, willing and able to participate in the process of revitalizing Harlem through economic empowerment. We pledged our resources, facilities, employees, and our business skills to the success of that endeavor. But our agenda did not happen to fall in line with the Empowerment Zone's agenda for gentrification of the Greater Harlem Community's business strip.

In April of 1994 WISE held a press conference entitled, *Female Entrepreneurs Proclaim Economic Emancipation In Harlem* at the Adam Clayton Powell, Jr. State Office Building in Harlem. We announced our support of Harlem's Empowerment Zone and asked for active participation in its planning and establishment. We announced that we would be lobbying for an African-American female to be chosen to control the disbursement of these loans; to ensure that the history of systematic exclusion of women from access to these loans would not be repeated. We did get an African-American female, but we forgot about classism, and we forgot that some of our people thought that we, who provided their jobs, were not worthy of ownership.

At that press conference I gave a statement, which read:

> *"The economic and social plight of the small businesses and people of Harlem must be dealt with if there is going to be any change for Harlem. We will appeal for specific provisions that will make allocations of loans available to female entrepreneurs not based solely on financial history, but also on the feasibility of the businesses or business plans, and the total benefits to be gained by the community through the development of these businesses. This specific vision is the result of our experience of being systematically denied loans and contracts in the past."*

It was commonly recognized that in this era of downsizing, cut-backs, and exporting of jobs outside U.S. borders by large corporations, small businesses were being looked to for the future growth of the national economy. In Harlem, where one-third of small businesses were owned by African-American women employing Harlem residents, WISE contended that we deserved at least as much attention from the EZ as was given to Yankee Stadium!

You can determine for yourself what support we have gotten in our efforts to maintain business in Harlem's Empowerment Zone. Black-owned Georgie's Bakery and Donut Shop, which had been in business for over 35 years and which got no support from the EZ, has closed. Krispy Kreme (a donut chain which makes donuts similar to Georgie's) came to 125th Street months before Georgie's closed, supported by the EZ. Copeland's Country Kitchen on 125th Street was suddenly hit with a $31,000 per month rent. The landlord was McDonald's. We still eat their burgers, and Mr. Copeland had to fire sixty African-American workers whom he had spent money to train. There was no help from the EZ or others in power, to rectify this situation. Business after African-American business has closed down—forced out by "empowered" corporations who hire African-Americans to do their dirty work for them; closing our businesses and making excuses, blaming the victims for being in the position to be victimized.

The Empowerment Zone's admitted philosophy of "empowering" our people is to bring in large corporations to create jobs, while our philosophy is to support ownership in the community to create wealth, security and a strong social culture. As jobs are very much needed, you can see how their philosophy may be attractive to people, but at what price? Gentrification so often looks attractive. It promises clean, well-lit, well-kept streets. It promises a daily visage of people walking to and from work and school, people shopping, etc.,—instead of hanging out on corners with no place to go. Can we not conceive of a Harlem which looks and feels as I have described without gentrification? Without the creation of a permanent underclass of poor workers, criminals and homeless, hopeless souls?

Dorothy Pitman Hughes welcomes the Honorable Percy Sutton, Assembleyman Keith Wright, and Film & Television Producer Carol Jenkins to her Sojourner Bed and Breakfast Fundraiser at Avery Fisher Hall.

Chapter Seven
My "EZ" Introduction

"They don't lynch darkies in America anymore."

—*Ken Hamblin, Feb. 27, 1994*

I first became aware of the Empowerment Zone concept and legislation in this way: I received a call from a person referred to me by someone whom I consider one of my best friends. The caller described himself as a "lawyer" and asked if I could be of assistance to two men from California who would be coming to Harlem to look at it in relation to the development of a plan called, "Vision Harlem". In order to plan for the future of Harlem, they would have to really *see* Harlem—not as tourists or being viewed as either the "vicious white male" or as "integrationists". "So, Dorothy, can you help? Your friend said if anyone could show us the real deal, you could." And so I became a paid consultant for what I later learned was a study of Harlem as a possible Empowerment Zone.

As we traveled throughout Harlem, we saw the ruins of Harlem's housing stock and the decay of its infrastructure. In every area where there were concentrations of poor people we saw a lack of sanitation and garbage pick-up, substance abuse and trafficking, an intense police presence with more ticketing of cars than in other residential areas of the city, and many homeowners and businesses being ticketed for the constant flow of garbage accumulating outside their doors due to the lack of sanitation service. We documented over 1,000 street vendors on 125th Street, from 1st Avenue to Broadway. We saw the absence of African-American ownership, the presence of gentrification, and we took a look at politics in the raw.

Many have misunderstood the role of the street vendors. Many well intentioned people, who stood up for the vendors when the business owners were fighting for their removal to an "open-air market" set up specifically for them, did not realize that the vendors were being used to create an atmosphere of confusion and squalor so that gentrification could be completed using the federal, state and city funds that were legislated to "empower" us. They thought that the plan was to empower from the bottom up, not from the top down, as is taking place. The number of vendors grew to the point where they were literally blocking the pedestrians' view of the storefront windows, and causing stores on the avenue to lose business. On Wednesdays we could see the real owners of the street goods—which were being sold by mostly Africans—come to 125th Street, open up folding chairs, collect their money from the vendors and then get back in their cars; taking their money back to their communities. If you have been through, or have any understanding of sharecropping in the South, you will recognize that what occurred on 125th Street was more of the same.

With these two white men, I gained entrance to certain places which I would have otherwise been barred from. We met with heads of corporations, universities and other organizations. We met with the bar association, where a presentation of the project was made that was quite different from the presentation given at an earlier meeting with the community. We met during the day with community groups and then later, over dinner in a downtown hotel, with corporate heads, etc., and *there* the real decisions would be made. I began to see clearly that the agenda of this bold, new project was not empowerment but gentrification.

The plan for Harlem to enter the competition for an Empowerment Zone was well underway. The agency that would house and develop the project was naturally "HUDC" Harlem Urban Development Corporation. Staff had been decided upon. The non-profit, business and social service committees were formed.

Having been on the "Vision Harlem" research team, I had the opportunity to take a close look at the committee that would be responsible for economic development. I felt that as one of Harlem's black, female business owners, I should be on the EZ's Economic Empowerment Planning Committee. I requested a seat but was told the committee was already complete. Knowing that this was the key committee to work from on behalf of black business, I decided that I would insist on my being placed on it.

I wrote my congressman, Congressman Rangel, who was the "father" of the Empowerment Zone plan for Harlem and one of the creators of the legislation that made it possible for other states to have Empowerment Zones. I then called a meeting of WISE. Seven women from the group were selected to attend a meeting with the Congressman. We all put $100 into the development of a joint proposal showing why our businesses should have representation on the Economic Empowerment Planning Committee of the EZ. We met with Congressman Rangel, who agreed, and I was chosen by the group to represent us.

Out of our involvement on the committee came the concept of the Business Resource and Investment Service Center (BRISC). The agency, which was within the Upper Manhattan (Harlem) Empowerment Zone Administration, was to work with and initially prepare small businesses for loans and/or grants through the EZ operations. Not only did we provide the EZ with a way to include small business in the mix, *to co-exist with their intended gentrification process*, but we also helped in providing them with their director of BRISC; as I believe that Herman Velasquez got at *least* a bit of exposure in the EZ community while he was working with me on the business plan that I was making to the EZ.

We all agreed, at the time, that our working together was resulting in some wonderful possibilities. I chose to believe that Herman, who was in charge of the funding for small businesses, would approve a loan to H.O.S., Inc. based on the *wonderful business plan he helped me to produce*. But, those are the breaks when one is black and female in business and refuses to front for white males.

What follows is a synopsis of our business plan, which includes Letters of Support, and letters acknowledging the kinds of dollars being spent outside the community. Following the condensed proposal, you will see the form letter sent to me by the Director of the EZ, denying assistance to H.O.S., Inc. (Note the reason stated).

Dorothy Pitman Hughes with television host, author and radio talk show host Tony Brown and Nurideen Muhammad after speaking at the Empowerment Seminar in Newark, New Jersey.

HARLEM OFFICE SUPPLY, Inc.

Business Plan

Dorothy Pitman Hughes
President & C.E.O.
Harlem Office Supply, Inc.
6 East 125th Street
New York, New York 10035
Phone: 212-427-3540/427-3615
Fax: 212-427-3816

This document is for background information only and is not to be construed as either a private or public offering.

Executive Summary

Located at 6 East 125th Street, the heart of the Harlem community's bustling commercial center, Harlem Office Supply, Inc. (HOS) was incorporated on May 15, 1992. This attractive and neatly kept store has enjoyed steady sales growth by offering first quality office products at reasonable prices, and copying services to small and medium-sized businesses, government offices, schools, and the general public.

With 1,110 square feet of selling space and additional office and storage space, the business offers over 25,000 inventory items. The business's copy center offers high volume photocopying, word processing, typesetting, offset printing, and binding services. In 1994, the income after taxes was $19,500. For the first five months of 1995, the company has generated $151,630 in sales with a net income of $8,856. Annualization of the sales thus far in 1995, would mean an increase of 30% over 1994.

HOS competes through quality of its service, which includes free delivery for customers in the store's primary market area. (Deliveries to customers outside the primary market area are made by United Parcel Service.) HOS has identified core items that are most price sensitive, and keeps those items close in price to the large chains. The business's competitive advantage lies in its ability to provide personalized service while offering its local customers a chance to spend dollars within the community and thereby contribute to the community's overall economic health. The incentive to spend dollars with a locally owned business has made it possible for the company to collect letters of commitment for future purchases representing $296,000 in new annual business. The company plans to install an advanced point-of-sale computer system that will make it possible to be even more responsive to customer needs and strengthen its marketing efforts throughout Federal Empowerment Zones and Enterprising Communities.

Having profitably served HOS since its inception, Dorothy Pitman Hughes continues to serve as the company's President and C.E.O. Ms. Hughes has been an owner and operator of new enterprises for more than twenty-five years. Ms. Hughes is an individual of tremendous energy and vision, and has devoted considerable time to community affairs while growing her various enterprises. The rest of the management team members are described in the Management & Organization section of this plan. The company is further supported by the CPA firm of Seidel, Kessler, Blum & Company, P.C., Sperber, Denenberg, Barany, P.C., Attorneys at Law, and Reginald Oliver, President, On Target Information Services.

The company's current market area is the uptown section of Manhattan, including Harlem, Washington Heights, and Inwood. The greatest concentration of business, and therefore the company's primary market area, is Central Harlem where HOS is conveniently located. The businesses located in the area are mostly small and medium-sized businesses, with a notable number of large institutions. The business plans to increase its market penetration by continuing its extensive networking activities within the local business community. Market penetration is aided by the distribution of flyers throughout the community and catalogs at the store, during sales calls, and through direct mail. The store displays most of its inventory on the sales floor according to a company developed plan-o-gram.

The company's direct competition consists of two small companies located in the same zip code as HOS. University Student Supply is located at 1201 Amsterdam Avenue. The store reports annual sales of $200,000. Helen's Stationery, Inc. is located at 285 St. Nicholas Avenue and reports annual sales of $80,000. neither of these stores enjoys a significant competitive advantage of a higher profile location, larger selling space, and a greater variety of services. HOS may someday face a competitive challenge from a large office supply chain. HOS intends to meet this challenge with superior service and commitment to the community. The company is also exploring the possibility of some form of joint venture with a major chain and met with a major office supply chain in June 1995.

The Harlem community is gearing up for a ten year advance toward major economic change and an improved quality of life. HOS plans to continue playing a supporting role in the move toward economic stability. The Federal Empowerment Zone designation which includes Harlem will see the investment of $3.65 billion for the growth of business and job opportunities. The owner of HOS has long been involved in the movement that brought about the Empowerment Zone designation. While HOS stands to benefit substantially over the next ten years, the company's owner is one of many community leaders and business owners committed to seeing the Empowerment Zone becoming a rousing success in Harlem.

The company is currently seeking $360,000 in debt financing in order to undertake a major expansion and accommodate the new sales represented by the aforementioned letters of commitment. An infusion of capital will allow HOS to double the size of its current selling, office and storage space. The increased purchasing power will allow the company to maintain an inventory level sufficient to meet increasing customer demand while maintaining service quality, purchase a point-of-sale system, purchase a delivery van, and copying and printing equipment.

Management & Organization

The C.E.O.

The business's management team is headed by the company's President and C.E.O., Dorothy Pitman Hughes. The founder of the company, she has long been dedicated to creating better economic opportunities for her community, and has a long and varied history as a developer, organizer, and director of successful enterprises. Ms. Hughes has made major financial commitments to the development and expansion of HOS. Her investment includes ten years of planning and growing the business.

During the mayoralty of John Lindsay she founded and organized N.Y.C.'s Agency for Child Development, which provides care for 70,000 children daily and employs thousands. Ms. Hughes organized the first battered women's shelter in N.Y.C., has owned and operated three day care centers, and sponsored a successful youth entrepreneur apprentice project. She spent three years as a public speaker on the university circuit, been a substitute teacher on Social Change and Economic Parity at Columbia University for Professor Hamilton, been a teacher at the College of New Rochelle and City College, and received numerous Letters of Commendation and Awards. HOS is an expansion of Quick Copy service in Harlem which was owned and operated by Ms. Hughes from 1985 to 1991.

Ms Hughes is a member of the Stationer's Association of New York, the Harlem Empowerment Zone Economic Development Committee, the Harlem Business Alliance, Black Women Enterprises, the D.P.H. Entrepreneur Marketing Network, the National Black Women's Political Congress, the National Organization for Women, the National Council of Negro Women, and Women Initiating Self Empowerment.

C.E.O. Responsibilities

The C.E.O.'s responsibilities include oversight of planning, developing, and establishing of HOS's policies and objectives. The C.E.O. establishes staff responsibilities and procedures for attaining objectives. She reviews activity reports and financial statements to determine progress and revise objectives and plans accordingly. She evaluates staff member performance for compliance with established policies and objectives and their constitution in obtaining objectives. She plans and develops public relations policies designed to improve the company's image and relations with customers, employees, and the public. The C.E.O. oversees the work of outside specialists and approves all promotional materials. She is responsible for assessing future product development.

Product & Service Plan

Purpose of HOS Products & Services

HOS's products and services provide needed items to the small and mid-sized businesses, institutions, and the general public of Uptown Manhattan. Offering high quality, brand name products at reasonable prices, free local delivery, and the opportunity to access additional business services such as high volume copying, HOS is a convenient and reasonably priced vendor to its customers.

Products and Services

1. HOS carries over 25,000 inventory items including general supplies, office equipment, office furniture, and other business-related items. Those in the Uptown Manhattan area can avail themselves of the companies free deliveries.

2. The business's copy center offers high volume photo-copying, word processing, typesetting, offset printing, and binding services. The new equipment to be leased will increase the company's capacity to perform additional services such as color copying.

3. At the customer's request HOS will take over management of the company's supply cabinet and keep it permanently replenished. HOS will assess the kinds of supplies a company is using and recommend better products to improve its image and efficiency. With HOS as their supplier, customers need not to have someone at their company to deal with these issues.

Unique Features

HOS is Uptown Manhattan's only full-service supplier of office products, business related items, and business services. HOS enjoys the highest profile location of any competitor within its primary market area and has the largest selling space. The company has recently put an 800 phone number in place for the convenience of customers making inquiries or placing orders by phone.

Stage Of Development

At this time HOS is a $363,000 a year company poised for a major expansion. Since 1992, the company has been building customer loyalty and has recently collected letters of intent from potential customers for future purchases totaling $296,000. The company is seeking to quickly move to annual sales exceeding $1 million. At this time, the company is exploring the possibility of a joint venture or cooperative arrangement with a major office supply chain and has begun discussing the possibility with one such chain. In order to bring the business to the next stage of development the company will need the commitment of $360,000 in debt financing.

Limitations and Liabilities

Annual insurance expenses of $6000 have been budgeted to include a full package of business insurance. This package will cover business property, property off-premises, business interruption, money and securities, outdoor signs, plate glass, valuable papers, accounts receivable, property of others, computer hardware and software, employee dishonesty, commercial general liability, product losses, and fire damage.

Financial Controls

The business will employ the use of an advanced point-of-sale computer system which has been budgeted at $15,000. Calling on their experience with this same business type, the company CPA's will work with computer consultants to establish a solid financial control system which will track inventory, sales orders, accounts receivable, accounts payable and payroll.

Marketing Plan

Industry Profile

According to U.S. Department of Commerce statistics, the aggregate dollar amount of manufacturer's shipments of many of the categories of office products offered by HOS, exclusive of distributor and retail price mark-ups, is approximately $38 billion annually. Sales of office products in the United states are made primarily through office products dealers. These dealers generally operate one or more retail stores and utilize a central warehouse facility. The industry is highly fragmented with only a few regional or national chains. Dealers purchase a significant proportion of their merchandise from manufacturers. Goods purchased at the distributor's wholesale prices are marked up to provide a profit to the distributor. Dealers usually offer credit terms to their business customers. HOS is charged close to full price due to lack of credit line and the young age of the company.

Competition Profile

HOS's direct competition is two small stationery stores located in the nearby West Harlem zip code 10027. University Student Supply is located at 1201 Amsterdam Avenue. The store reports annual sales of $200,000. Started in 1992, the business is a proprietorship renting a single 800 square foot storefront, and reports three employees, up from one employee three years ago. Besides stationery the store sells gifts, novelties, souvenirs, and computer software and accessories. Helen's Stationery, Inc. is located at 285 St. Nicholas Avenue and reports annual sales of $80,000. Started in 1980, the business reports 2 employees and zero growth from five years ago. Neither of these stores enjoys a significant competitive advantage in variety of merchandise, purchasing power, pricing, or quality of service. HOS enjoys a higher profile location, larger selling space, and a greater variety of services. HOS may someday face a competitive challenge from a large office supply chain, against which it will have difficulty competing on price due to the greater purchasing power of the chain. HOS is now exploring the possibility of a joint venture or other cooperative arrangement with a major chain. If an acceptable arrangement with a major chain cannot be achieved, HOS intends to meet this challenge with the excellence of its customer service, and its commitment to improving economic opportunity within the community.

Walk-In Customer Profile

The primary source of walk-in trade for HOS is the residents of Community District 10 of Manhattan. Community District 10 is home to 99,519 residents. The racial composition is 87.5% African-American, 10.1% Hispanic, and 1.5% white. The median household income is $13,252 compared with the city-wide figure of $29,823. Almost 40% of area residents live below the poverty line. Additional walk-in traffic is drawn from neighboring Community Districts 9 and 11. Community District 9 is home to

106,978 residents. The racial composition is 39.1% African-American, 36.1% Hispanic, and 19.5% white. The median household income is $20,775. Community District 11 is home to 110,508 residents. The racial composition is 38.9% African-American, 51.9% Hispanic, and 7.1% white.

Customer Benefits

Local area residents, businesses, and institutions benefit from HOS's offering of high quality products at everyday low prices. A further benefit is the knowledge that the customer is spending his/her dollars at a business owned by a community resident committed to hiring from the local community, providing opportunities for advancement, and entrpreneurial training.

Target Market Profile

The target market for the office products and business related services offered by HOS is the businesses and institutions located in zip code 10027, near where the HOS store is located: boundaries are Fifth Avenue to the Hudson River, from West 117th Street to West 134th Street. According to Dun & Bradstreet, the area is home to 504 service companies, 281 retailers, 81 companies in the finance, insurance, and real estate industries, 57 wholesalers, 31 manufacturers, and 30 construction companies. Dun & Bradstreet also states that within zip code 10027 there are 92 community-based organizations, 40 colleges and universities, and 2 hospitals.

Beyond the aforementioned Zip Code HOS targets all businesses and institutions within the Federal Empowerment Zone, which covers all of Upper Manhattan and the South Bronx. The business has mapped information which identifies primary and secondary business prospects, and competitor business locations for the products and services offered by HOS.

Market Penetration

Currently, HOS achieves market penetration in two primary ways, through its high profile location and the networking efforts of the company's C.E.O. The store's East 125th Street location has seen dramatic improvement. A complete street reconstruction has been completed. With its brick paving, traffic lighting replacement and other improvements, the busy commercial hub has undergone a striking facelift. The location is at the heart of the 125th Street Business Improvement District which is responsible for the maintenance of the improvements, the cleanliness of the commercial strip, and the promotion of the District's business.

The company's C.E.O., Dorothy Pitman Hughes has long been active in the Harlem community. Currently, she is a member of the Harlem Empowerment Zone Economic Development Committee, the Harlem Business Alliance, and is President of the D.P.H. Entrepreneur to Entrepreneur Marketing Network, an organization of small business owners, including home-based businesses.

Additional market penetration is achieved by the distribution of catalogs at the store and during sales calls, the distribution of flyers throughout the community, limited direct mail, and limited advertising in local publications. The store displays most of its inventory on the sales floor according to a company developed plan-o-gram. The company will double the size of its store by leasing adjacent storefront, allowing the business to enhance the volume and variety of its inventory on display. A major change will be the company's $26,000 budget for advertising and promotion, or 4% of sales. This money will be used to increase the company's printing and distribution of marketing materials, expand the reach and frequency of its now severely limited advertising, and strengthen its ties and commitment to the community by being a sponsor of community events.

The company is presently looking to enlist the services of an experienced Marketing Consultant specializing in marketing strategies with emphasis on sales and distribution. In order to benefit from the services of such a consultant HOS has budgeted $12,000 in year 1 of the Financial Projections. The company will begin its search for the best matched consultant by meeting with the small business consulting department of Arthur Andersen & Company and organizations of similar reputation.

Hours of Operation

To provide maximum convenience for its customers the HOS store is open seven days a week. The hours of operation are from 8:30 AM to 9:30 PM Monday through Friday, 9:00 AM to 8:30 PM on Saturday, and 11:00AM to 7:30 PM on Sunday.

Financial Plan

Assumptions

Financial Requirements

1. All line items listed under Current Value represent the stated value on the corporation's most recent Balance Sheet, less accumulated depreciation and amortization.

2. The $73,000 for additional Machinery & Equipment represents the $15,000 for the purchase price of a point-of-sale computer system, the installation of the hardware and software, and the computer consulting costs associated with implementation and staff training. The remaining dollars will be used to purchase a Xerox 5385 Copier for $30,000, and a Xerox 5765 Edit Color Copier for $28,000.

3. The $10,000 for additional Furniture & Fixtures represents the purchase of shelving, light fixtures, and furniture for the additional space the business will be leasing.

4. The $57,190 for Leasehold Improvements represents the improvements to the additional space and the removal of the wall now between two spaces. The cost was estimated at 435 per square foot for the additional 1,364 square feet.

5. The $8,000 for a Delivery Van represents the purchase price of a previously owned vehicle.

6. The additional $10,033.32 for Deposits represents an additional deposit of two months rent for the additional space.

7. The $80,000 for Inventory represents the purchase of $35,000 in office supply inventory, $25,000 for art supplies, $10,000 for items for churches, and $10,000 for business related legal forms.

8. The $75,000 Cash in Bank represents additional working capital to meet the company's operating expenses during expansion. The $50,000 Deposits for Credit will be used to establish credit lines with manufacturers to be suppliers to HOS.

OPERATING PRO FORMA

1. The $650,000 in Sales includes the current annualized sales level of $364,000 plus $296,000 to account for the company's continued sales growth supported by letters from purchasers included in the Appendix of this plan.

2. The 18.6% Cost of Sales is based on the company's experience since its inception.

3. A Schedule of Salaries & Wages is included in the Financial Projections.

4. The $109,220 for Rent represents the monthly payment of $4,085 for the current store space and $5,016.66 for the additional 1,720 square feet.

5. The $9,500 for Utilities and the $14,000 for Telephone are based on the company's past experience.

6. The $4,000 for Maintenance represents the company's expenses for repairs and cleaning of the company's rented space.

7. The $4,200 for Repairs & Maintenance represents the cost for equipment service contracts plus miscellaneous repairs to the company's plant and equipment.

Cash Flow Projections

1. The monthly figures for Expected Cash Revenue was based on a slowly increasing rate of monthly sales as a percentage of annual sales, from 5% to 10%, and an average collection period of 30 days.

2. Operating Disbursements assume that operating expenses will remain largely fixed, regardless of sales performance.

3. Non-Operating Disbursements represent inventory replacement, the payment of past payables minus the collection of past receivables, and the payment of corporate income taxes minus EZ tax credits.

4. Loan Payments represent the monthly payment of principal and interest on a $360,000 loan at 11% interest, over an 8 year term.

Harlem Office Supply, Inc.
Projected Revenue & Expenses

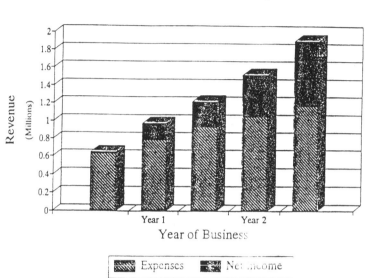

Dorothy Pitman Hughes is congratulated by Adam Clayton Powell III after her one woman show "Herstory in Black."

State of New York
Executive Department
Division of Human Rights
55 West 123 Street. 13th Fl.
New York NY 10027

Christian J. Nelson   Voice: (212) 961-4566
Senior Budgeting Analyst   Fax: (212) 961-8552

February 14, 1994

Phyllis Shelton
Harlem Office Supplies, Inc.,
Empowerment Marketing Specialist
121 W. 125th Street
New York, NY 10027

Dear Ms. Shelton:

Thank you for your letter concerning Harlem Office Supplies, Inc. and the challenges faced by businesses in the designated Empowerment Zone.

As you might know, the New York State Division of Human Rights does presently purchase some office supplies from Harlem Office Supplies, Inc. The Division selects Harlem Office Supplies, Inc. when the supplies we need are not under state contract or when we need supplies quickly. That fact that your business excepts a New York State Purchase Order makes it very easy for the Division to buy at your store.

In response to your letter, the Division will continue to purchase some office supplies from Harlem Office Supplies, Inc., at a competitive price.

If you have any questions please do not hesitate to call me

Sincerely,

Chris Nelson
cc   Jane Rubin

New York Post, Thursday, April 21, 1994

Bizwomen: Zone may leave us with zip

By Christopher Policano

A group of nearly 100 local businesswomen yesterday expressed fear they will be overlooked when Harlem is designated a federal empowerment zone.

Clearly frustrated by the historical obstacles they have faced in securing credit, the women called for a third of the federal aid expected for the zone to be set aside for small business loans.

"At least 15 community women have lost their homes trying to stay in business," said Dorothy Pitman Hughes, owner of Harlem Office Supply Corp. and president of a new community group called Women Initiating Self-Empowerment.

"We put our money into the banks and then we can't get it out."

Hughes also asked that a minority woman be hired to oversee loan disbursement.

But a spokeswoman for the Harlem Urban Development Corp., a non-profit group that has been designated to prepare the city's application for the zone, said the group was way ahead of the game.

"We have not even submitted the application, and you should never assume anything," said HUDC spokesperson Sam Mattingly.

"The money is to help the community in areas that have been neglected, such as child care and other human services."

Mattingly said small businesses, such as Hughes', in the zone will be helped by tax credits and tax-exempt financing.

Harlem, Washington Heights and a portion of the South Bronx around Yankee Stadium were recently designated as the city's entry in the competition for $100 million in federal inner-city improvement funds over two years.

Only six zones in urban areas across the country will be chosen.

HUDC will submit the application by the end of June, with input from local community and business groups.

New York is considered a favorite for funding because Rep. Charles Rangel, chairman of the powerful Ways and Means Committee, sponsored the legislation that created the zones.

"I cannot think of anything more important than the creation and maintenance of small business," Rangel said.

"Their problem is a real one—the inability to get capital. But this is not a grant program."

Hughes countered: "We are the largest group of employers in the area, and we provide jobs for hundreds of community residents."

June 28, 1994

To: Women of W.I.S.E.

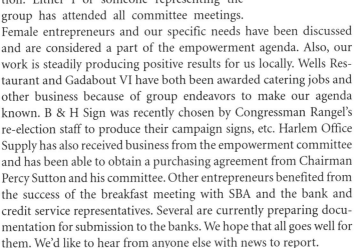

Although we must keep working on this project, I am glad to report that our platform has been addressed in the empowerment application. Either I or someone representing the group has attended all committee meetings. Female entrepreneurs and our specific needs have been discussed and are considered a part of the empowerment agenda. Also, our work is steadily producing positive results for us locally. Wells Restaurant and Gadabout VI have both been awarded catering jobs and other business because of group endeavors to make our agenda known. B & H Sign was recently chosen by Congressman Rangel's re-election staff to produce their campaign signs, etc. Harlem Office Supply has also received business from the empowerment committee and has been able to obtain a purchasing agreement from Chairman Percy Sutton and his committee. Other entrepreneurs benefited from the success of the breakfast meeting with SBA and the bank and credit service representatives. Several are currently preparing documentation for submission to the banks. We hope that all goes well for them. We'd like to hear from anyone else with news to report.

Due to our press conference, our presence was requested at a state assembly conference held by a committee headed by Bronx Assemblyman Arilia Green. The topic of discussion was on small businesses and how the legislature can better assist them. There was in depth dialogue on the unique agenda of African-American businesswomen. Assemblywoman Green was most responsive to the W.I.S.E. platform and her interest in helping African -American women seems to be genuine.

The efforts of W.I.S.E. are also being recognized on the federal level. A report on our press conference and its agenda was reported to Congress by Congresswoman Maxine Waters. Also, Senator Carol Mosely Braun from Chicago has expressed interest in what we're doing and her willingness to help. Our network has been greatly strengthened by the relationships we've developed with other organizations such as BWE, Ms. Foundation, AWED, and Chemical Bank.

We have already proven that working together we can produce results and be successful. To continue on, everyone must stay involved and informed. The cost of past work, i.e. press conference, breakfast meeting, written literature, publicity, totaled $4,872.00 and DPH Marketing Network has basically carried the financial load. Outside funding which was promised never materialized. Membership fees did not cover even a quarter of the amount needed to finance our work since DPH does not have money, it became necessary to use funds from Harlem Office Supply. I am committed to our cause and will do all I can to help us to be successful; but, I am not able to cover the bulk of expenses alone. We must pay for so many things to keep our work progressing. To send out this update alone, there is the costs of paper, printing, a typist, a writer, stamps, envelopes and more. There is no group fund for such expenses. Therefore, to help cover costs, we are planning several fundraisers. The first is being planned for Thursday, July 14, 1994. It will be a mystical evening of networking and socializing at the Enchanted Restaurant.

Tickets will cost $25.00. Anyone interested in helping out can contact my business office. Finally, although some services (consultations, writing, typing, etc.) carry a fee, we are always available for assistance with your entrepreneurial endeavors.

Membership cards can be obtained at Harlem Office Supply, Inc.

Respectfully,

Dorothy P. Hughes
D.P.H. Marketing Network

The City College
of The City University of New York
Convent Ave. at 138 St
New York, New York 10031

Office Of The President

April 11, 1995

Ms. Dorothy Pitman Hughes
Harlem Office Supplies, Inc.
121 West 125th Street
New York, NY 10027

Dear Ms. Hughes:

The City College of New York has been actively supporting the Harlem Empowerment Zone Initiative under the leadership of Congressman Charles Rangel.

We understand that a major focus of the Empowerment Zone Initiative is business growth and development. In that light I would like to assure you that I will encourage the various components of the College to provide business opportunities to yours and other local competitive business that meet the necessary State vendor criteria that the College is obligated to abide by.

In looking at the College office supply needs, we purchase an estimated amount of $80,000 of 8 1/2 x 11 20 lb stock paper each year. This could be the first area of discussion as to how we could utilize your services if all of the necessary vendor-purchasing procedures meet State guidelines.

I would suggest that you continue to work with Mr. Tony Rogers, the College's Director of External Relations, who will assist you in meeting the necessary College personnel that will provide you with vendor-purchasing procedures.

I wish you the best of luck in your business development endeavors.

Sincerely,

Yolanda T Moses, President

The W.I.S.E. Plan for Economic Development

By Claudette Spence

A Harlem-based group of African American female entrepreneurs recently called a press conference to announce their intent to remain a strong economic force in Harlem and in the city of New York through proactive participation in Harlem's Empowerment Zone plan.

Led by Dorothy Pitman Hughes, owner of Harlem Office Supplies and founder of D.P.H. Marketing Network/Women Initiating Self-Empowerment (WISE), the group highlighted the barriers to women's successful entry and longevity in business as well as their attempts to be a more viable economic force in the community.

"Forty seven percent of small businesses in Harlem are minority owned and 33% of all businesses are owned by women," said Hughes. Small businesses in Harlem create employment for Harlemites and Hughes continued, "I think we deserve as much attention as Yankee Stadium in the Empowerment Zone of the City." In the Economic Zone bill sponsored by Congressman Charles Rangel. $300 million is committed to Harlem. The over 100 women entrepreneurs in attendance want to have $33,000,000 of the first $100,000,000 committed to the strengthening of their capacities to enable them to be competitive businesses and employers.

"Small businesses in Harlem must have access to low-interest loans to do business, help them to get health plans for their employees and pay these employees a wage on which they can live," Hughes noted.

Hughes serves on the Economic Development Work Committee of the Empowerment Zone, working to ensure that the vision becomes a reality and that people of the community are indeed empowered by the plan. For Hughes this means seeing to it that businesses are strengthened and Harlem residents, particularly young people, will gain employment.

An important committee on which small business people should serve is the committee responsible for disbursing the funds. For further information about the Empowerment Zone plan contact the office of the Harlem Urban Development Corporation 212-961-4100.

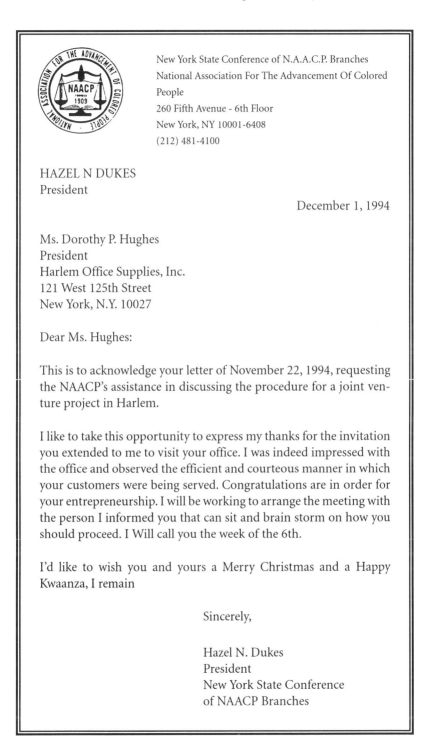

New York State Conference of N.A.A.C.P. Branches
National Association For The Advancement Of Colored
People
260 Fifth Avenue - 6th Floor
New York, NY 10001-6408
(212) 481-4100

HAZEL N DUKES
President

December 1, 1994

Ms. Dorothy P. Hughes
President
Harlem Office Supplies, Inc.
121 West 125th Street
New York, N.Y. 10027

Dear Ms. Hughes:

This is to acknowledge your letter of November 22, 1994, requesting the NAACP's assistance in discussing the procedure for a joint venture project in Harlem.

I like to take this opportunity to express my thanks for the invitation you extended to me to visit your office. I was indeed impressed with the office and observed the efficient and courteous manner in which your customers were being served. Congratulations are in order for your entrepreneurship. I will be working to arrange the meeting with the person I informed you that can sit and brain storm on how you should proceed. I Will call you the week of the 6th.

I'd like to wish you and yours a Merry Christmas and a Happy Kwaanza, I remain

Sincerely,

Hazel N. Dukes
President
New York State Conference
of NAACP Branches

Harlem Office Supplies, Inc.
121 West 125th Street
New York, NY 10027

THOMAS G. STEMBERG
Chief Executive Officer
Staples, Inc.
100 Pennsylvania Avenue
P.O. Box 857
Framingham, Massachusetts 01701

Dear Mr. Stemberg:

Harlem, New York, was recently designated as one of the federal government's Empowerment Zones (EZ). This legislation is designed for expanding existing community businesses and bringing in new businesses in order to create and develop economic growth and empowerment for more people within the community.

As owner and operator of Harlem Office Supplies, Inc., I have always employed and apprenticed area residents who would otherwise have remained jobless. as a member of the EZ's Economic Development Committee, I also helped to develop the proposal that resulted in the choosing of Harlem as an EZ. I am the only African-American female in the state of New York with this kind of business, and the first in its 89-year history to be accepted into the Stationers' Association of New York. As a result, all of the major businesses in Harlem are giving the support needed to make Harlem Office Supplies, Inc. the central source for quality office furniture, equipment and supplies within the EZ. I am the only office supply business applying to the Empowerment Committee for expansion.

At the suggestion of some community leaders, I am writing to request a meeting with you to discuss the possibilities of exclusive franchise arrangements between Staples, Inc., and Harlem Office Supplies, Inc. As a member of the EZ, I will have access to low-interest loans, tax abatements and other EZ support systems. These advantages, combined with the magnitude of commercial development that will soon begin in Harlem, would make this a very lucrative venture for both of us.

Due to the timeliness of my proposal to be submitted to the Empowerment Committee in mid-February, I would appreciate a meeting with you at your earliest convenience, as I would like to include the results of my communications with you, and any possible relationship.

I look forward to meeting with you soon.

Respectfully,

DOROTHY PITMAN HUGHES
President

HARLEM CDC

March 15, 1996

Ms. Dorothy Pitman Hughes
Harlem Office Supplies, Inc.
121 West 125th Street
Store #6
New York, NY 10027

Dear Ms. Hughes:

Per my meeting with Ms. Beverly Griggsby on this past Monday, I have again recalculated the arrears owed by Harlem Office Supplies ("HOS"). The outstanding amount of arrears owed by HOS is $29,887.80. This amount was arrived at by giving credit for $2,450.00 from the May 18, 1992 check in the amount of $7,350.00 of which $2,450.00 was for rent and the rest for security deposit. All past credits we have discussed prior to this date are included in the amount of arrears.

On October 20, 1993 HOS increased its $4,900.00 security deposit by $4,631.66 due to its moving to a larger store for a total of $9531.66. HOS's rent will now be $3,562.50 per month, not including arrears payments. The security deposit of two months is $7125.00. I have included in arrears credit the $2,406.66 in excess security deposit. This is of course included in the above calculations.

As Harlem CDC agreed to earlier, we will reduce the arrears by 25% for a total outstanding arrears of $22,415.85. The arrears ears must be paid over the remaining term of the lease of 34 months (starting January 1, 1996) HOS's lease expires on October 31, 1998. The monthly amount will be $659.29 ($22,415.85 divided by 34 = $659.29) Total monthly rent due from January 1, 1996 through the end of the lease is $4,221.79 monthly which includes all arrears due.

Monies due Harlem CDC from HOS for January, February and March, 1996 are $ 12,665.37. We are holding HOS's February, 1996 check in the amount of $3,500.00 and will deposit ft. Please submit a check in the amount of $9165.37.

The proposal Harlem CDC has offered will save Harlem Office Supplies over $75,000.00 over the remaining term of the original lease which you signed, and over $8,000 for your arrears ears for a total savings of over $83,000.00. Harlem CDC will not charge interest or late penalties on the arrearage.

It is unfortunate that the rental problem was not resolved by the prior corporation. Harlem CDC is pleased we could be helpful in resolving these outstanding issues we look forward to your continued tenancy.

Sincerely,

Stephen B. Parnes
Director
Commercial Development

cc: Richard Eaddy
Warren S. Whitlock

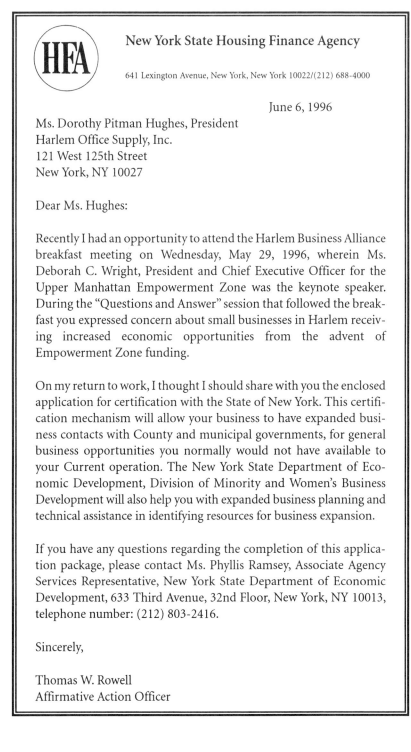

New York State Housing Finance Agency

641 Lexington Avenue, New York, New York 10022/(212) 688-4000

June 6, 1996

Ms. Dorothy Pitman Hughes, President
Harlem Office Supply, Inc.
121 West 125th Street
New York, NY 10027

Dear Ms. Hughes:

Recently I had an opportunity to attend the Harlem Business Alliance breakfast meeting on Wednesday, May 29, 1996, wherein Ms. Deborah C. Wright, President and Chief Executive Officer for the Upper Manhattan Empowerment Zone was the keynote speaker. During the "Questions and Answer" session that followed the breakfast you expressed concern about small businesses in Harlem receiving increased economic opportunities from the advent of Empowerment Zone funding.

On my return to work, I thought I should share with you the enclosed application for certification with the State of New York. This certification mechanism will allow your business to have expanded business contacts with County and municipal governments, for general business opportunities you normally would not have available to your Current operation. The New York State Department of Economic Development, Division of Minority and Women's Business Development will also help you with expanded business planning and technical assistance in identifying resources for business expansion.

If you have any questions regarding the completion of this application package, please contact Ms. Phyllis Ramsey, Associate Agency Services Representative, New York State Department of Economic Development, 633 Third Avenue, 32nd Floor, New York, NY 10013, telephone number: (212) 803-2416.

Sincerely,

Thomas W. Rowell
Affirmative Action Officer

UPPER MANHATTAN EMPOWERMENT ZONE
DEVELOPMENT CORPORATION
163 West 12tth Street, Suite 1204
New York, NY 10027
Tel: (212) 932-1902 Fax: (212) 932-1907

October 4, 1996

Ms. Dorothy P. Hughes
Harlem Office Supply, Inc.
121 West 125th St.
New York, NY 10027

Re: Proposal to Empowerment Zone

Dear Ms. Hughes:

Thank you for submitting your proposal to the Upper Manhattan Empowerment Zone Development Corporation ("UMEZDC"). During our first funding round, we received many compelling ideas for redevelopment of the Empowerment Zone. We appreciate the time and interest you have put into the development of your proposal.

After careful review we have determined that your proposal to expand an existing business is incomplete in several fundamental areas. As such we are unable to fully evaluate the extent to which the proposal meets the Empowerment Zone Investment Criteria e.g., impact, feasibility, sustainability and a qualified team. We therefore believe your business would benefit from the assistance and resources provided by the Business Resource and Investment Service Center ("BRISC"). The BRISC, a subsidiary of the UMEZDC, opened on September 16, 1996. It was established to provide locally-based existing businesses mid start-ups with assistance in the development of business plans, marketing strategies, financial management and recordkeeping practices, and to improve or restore credit ratings, as well as other business planning tools. The BRISC will also, where appropriate, provide or direct businesses to available financing that has been elusive in our community. We have referred your proposal to the Executive Director of the BRISC for follow-up. Please call for an appointment and/or visit their state of the art library, equipped with business manuals and internet access. It is located at 271 West 125th Street, at the comer of Frederick Douglas Blvd., on the 2nd and 3rd floors.

Once again, we thank you for your continued interest in the Upper Manhattan Empowerment Zone.

Sincerely,
Deborah C. Wright, President & CEO
Upper Manhattan Empowerment Zone
Development Corporation

HARLEM OFFICE
SUPPLY INC.

October 28,1996

Ms. Deborah Wright
President & CEO
Upper Manhattan Empowerment Zone
Development Corporation
163 West 125th Street, Suite 1204
New York, N.Y. 10027

Re: Proposal to Empowerment Zone

Dear Ms. Wright:

I am writing in response to your letter of October 4, 1996, in which you rejected our Business Plan and Proposal for Harlem Office Supply, Inc., to the Empowerment Zone, and referred us to the Business Resource and Investment Service Center (BRISC) for assistance in the development of business plans, etc.

You are probably unaware that my proposal was in fact prepared in close collaboration with Mr. Herman Velasquez, the Executive Director of the BRISC, who spent from six to eight month's working with me developing the Harlem Office Supply Business Plan, including the detailed financial projections, marketing analyses and strategy and description of management and organization.

Further, the idea for the BRISC itself was suggested through the Economic Development Planning Committee of the Empowerment Zone chaired by Mr. George Weldon of the Harlem Business Alliance. I served on this committee, and brought this issue to the table on behalf of Women Initiating Self Empowerment (WISE). The fact that the concept of the BRISC was born in large part from information we submitted detailing our suffering, and experience of being excluded from obtaining assistance for our businesses was openly acknowledged and recorded by the committee. We outlined before the committee the idea that businesses in Harlem needed a walk-in resource center which understood what banks etc., are looking for from business applicants; with accountants, proposal writers, business plan writers, etc., to assist them. We called for "immediate provisions which allow us to transcend the burdens which hinder us."

Thank you for the advice in your letter; I have attempted to contact Mr. Velasquez to assist me in clarifying for you the areas of my proposal that you stated were incomplete: e.g., impact, feasibility, sustainability and a qualified team. Thus far I have been unsuccessful in three attempts to arrange a meeting with him. I would greatly appreciate your assistance in facilitating this meeting. Because of our past collaboration on my business plan, I am confident that Mr. Velasquez and I will be able to elucidate for you and the committee the points you raised, and thus enable you to reconsider Harlem Office Supply's application. I hope that upon further examination, you will find it sound and feasible.

With sincere regards,

Dorothy Pitman Hughes
President

cc: Cong. Charles B. Rangel
      Mr. Charles Gargano, Chmn., Emp. State Devel. Corp.
      Gov. George Pataki
      Mr. Richard Parsons, Chmn. of Bd., Emp. Zone Devel. Corp.

HARLEM OFFICE
SUPPLY INC.

November 3, 1996

Ms. Deborah Wright
President & CEO
Upper Manhattan Empowerment Zone
Development Corporation
163 West 125th Street, Suite 1204
New York, N.Y. 10027

Re: Proposal to Empowerment Zone

Dear Ms. Wright:

Your call to me on Friday was quite a surprise and your message to me was even more surprising. I was really taken back when you hung up your phone in the middle of my response to your statement. So that there is no continued misunderstanding, I repeat, I have not in the past, and will not in the future, spend time "trashing" you.

When you said that I "trashed" you to a reporter, I say again that is not true. As I told you, I had not mentioned your name or your position to any reporter. Yes, I did give the reporters the letter I received, as it was what I then thought was the basis for my not receiving financial support from the Empowerment Zone Board of Directors.

I asked for a loan, not a grant. And the letter I gave to the reporter was my only communication from the Empowerment Zone representatives.

I have now been informed by you that the real reason for denying me a loan you did not put in the letter because you did not want to put my business in the street. When I asked you the real reason, you said to me, "It's because you are not a good business person." I asked you how it is determined that I'm not a good business person. You stated that it is because I owe taxes and rent.

I asked you then, and I ask you now, to put that in writing to me. If the Board has denied a loan to me because I owe taxes and rent, I don't mind if you put that information in the streets. I have already told the press that I owe taxes and rent; I have also told them that if I was given a loan I would use other means to pay the taxes and keep the business going.

Again, I never mentioned your name or your position at the E.Z. I told one reporter that the E.Z. was a big help to H.O.S., because the E.Z. buys some products from us. The sign in my store window states: "THE E.Z. HAS NOT YET GIVEN ANY SUPPORT TO US, H.O.S., INC., THAT WOULD ALLOW US TO HIRE THE 260 APPLICANTS FOR JOBS ON FILE. PLEASE COME IN TO FIND OUT WHO WAS GIVEN THE MONEY, SO YOU CAN ASK THEM FOR JOBS."

I have worked in this community for 31 years. The last few years have been spent on my business and the planning committee for the Empowerment Zone. I feel that my contribution has helped to employ you as the Empowerment Zone President and C.E.O. When you were appointed, I cheered. It did not occur to me that I would find myself in a position where my freedom of speech and expression of my disappointment would be a reason for not getting support from you or the Board of Directors in the Empowerment Zone. I do feel that the 260 applicants for jobs that I saw will benefit from receiving the list of E.Z.-funded businesses and organizations. It is now public, but they might not have read it in the newspapers.

When you slammed your phone down, I was asking you if the E.Z. could possibly find a way to help me with H.O.S., Inc., so that we could meet all of our obligations and grow the business/jobs as intended.

I will still come to the BRISC as you first suggested, but if the reason for denying support is more of a personal nature I would like to meet with you and the Board to see if I can be helped to become a better business person.

Respectfully,

DOROTHY PITMAN HUGHES

January 29, 1997

Daily News Business
Harlem Copeland's gets McD shuffle

By Peter Grant
Daily News Business Writer

Ronald McDonald is giving the boot to Copeland's Country Kitchen, forcing the well-known Harlem eatery to close its 226-seat restaurant on 125th St. and lay off 60 workers.

The financially troubled Copeland's is set to shut its doors Friday on the expansion restaurant it opened in 1995 to cash in on the growing popularity of its smothered chicken, collard greens and jambalaya.

Copeland officials said the action is necessary because they could not negotiate a rent reduction from their landlord, McDonald's Corp.

"They want me out of the place," said Calvin Copeland, the restaurant's founder. "They told me to go skiing."

The original Copeland's on W. 145th St will remain open. But it, too, faces problems because of the company's bankruptcy filing last fall.

Copeland, who founded the first restaurant in 1960 with $750, said he cannot afford to pay McDonald's rent of $22,OOO a month for the 125th St location.

"The revenue has never been what I hoped it would be," he said yesterday.

Copeland also said that McDonald's rejected his efforts to get a rent reduction or bring in a partner to keep the restaurant open.

Copeland said McDonald's will now benefit from the $1.3 million in improvements that he made in the restaurant

Most of that money was borrowed with the help of state and federal programs designed to help small minority businessmen.

Laura Vega, a McDonald's spokeswoman, denied that the fast-food giant evicted Copeland.

"McDonald's has demonstrated a strong willingness to work with Mr. Copeland in the past," she said.

Vega pointed out that before the bankruptcy, McDonald's agreed to "four or five" changes in the lease terms, "all with options to benefit Mr. Copeland."

Vega would not comment, however, on Copeland's attempt to get a rent reduction in the wake of the bankruptcy filing. She said McDonald's, which already has an outlet nearby, has not decided what to do with the site.

The restaurant's closing marks a setback for efforts by Harlem business leaders to revitalize 125th St. The failure of the cafeteria-style eatery raises questions about the ability of new business ventures to attract sufficient revenue.

The dispute between Copeland's and McDonald's also could increase friction in the Harlem community between local business owners and the national retailers that are increasingly scouting the area for expansion possibilities.

Employees and customers of Copeland's said yesterday that its failure. demonstrated the difficulty posed for home-grown businesses by the influx of major corporations.

"The regular customers are shocked and angry," said Philip Bulgar, a food preparer at the restaurant.

"It seems as though it's going to be impossible for a small businessman to have a business in his own community."

McDonald's ended up as Copeland's landlord because the fast food chain planned to put an outlet at the location in the late 1980s. It decided to sublease the space to Copeland's after choosing a different site for its restaurant.

"They want me out of the place. They told me to go skiing."
CALVIN COPELAND, restaurant founder

UMEZ Continues Round One Funding

150 Upper Manhattan Businesses to Receive EZ Funding to Rehabilitate Stores; Alexander Doll Company, the EZ's Largest For-Profit Employer, is Strengthened for Future Growth.

On Friday, March 7, 1997, the Upper Manhattan Empowerment Zone Development Corporation's (UMEZDC) Board of Directors approved a second slate of projects for recommendation to the New York Empowerment Zone Corporation (NYEZ).

The projects were selected from proposals submitted to the EZ in August 1996. They include a commercial revitalization initiative to improve key shopping areas, a productivity package to retain and grow jobs at a major doll manufacturing company, a start-up reproduction/communications center, and a new videotape duplication center. Approximately 550 jobs will be retained or created as a result.

The $2.375 million commercial revitalization initiative is intended to create robust, safe and physically inviting commercial environments that can effectively compete for new commerce. The initial phase will assist 150 small merchants located on the major commercial corridors of Upper Manhattan: 116th, 125th, 159th, 181st and 207th streets. The three core objectives are: physical improvements, merchant technical assistance and capacity building for Business Improvement Districts and other merchants organizations.

The program will be implemented by four local organizations: the Local Development Corporation del Barrio in East Harlem; the 125th Street Business Improvement District in Central Harlem; and the Audubon Partnership for Economic Development, in collaboration with the 181st Street Business Improvement District and 159th Street Community League, in Washington Heights and Inwood.

The Alexander Doll Company (ADC), a manufacturer of collectible and specialty dolls, is the largest private for-profit employer in Upper Manhattan. ADC will receive up to $1.95 million in financing for employee productivity training, factory renovations and high technology computer equipment. EZ funds will permit the retention of 450 jobs, 90% of which are held by Upper Manhattan residents. This substantial investment will also put the company on solid footing for future growth which is expected to create 40-60 new jobs over the next three years.

Black United Fund of New York's CopyFast is a start-up business services venture in Central Harlem that will offer copying, computer and communications services, including Internet access, to residents and businesses in Upper Manhattan. The EZ is partnering with Carver Federal Savings Bank to provide a loan package of up to $200,000.

UMEZDC is also partnering with Citibank to finance the expansion of Broadway Video's duplication services division in West Harlem. The total project cost of approximately $ 1. 1 million includes capital for leasehold improvements and a technical training program for EZ residents. Local residents will be trained as operators and will learn production techniques in all aspects of videotape duplication, closed-captioning, standards conversion and distribution. Jose Rosado, a Broadway Video employee and resident of West Harlem, alerted the company to the Empowerment Zone and has been offered a management position at the new facility.

Proposals approved by the UMEZDC Board will be forwarded to Fran Reiter, Deputy Mayor for Economic Development and Planning and Chair of the New York Empowerment Zone Board; Charles Gargano, Chairman, Empire State Development Corporation; and Andrew Cuomo, Secretary of the Department of Housing and Urban Development, for approval. The NYEZ, comprised of federal, state and city representatives, will meet later this spring. Terms of each EZ financial participation are under negotiations.

Congressman Charles B. Rangel hailed the Board's actions as the latest victories for Upper Manhattan in the Empowerment Zone's first year of operation. "These projects mean jobs and increased commercial activity throughout the Empowerment Zone. I'm especially gratified by the assistance to small businesses along key shopping areas. These funds are a needed shot in the arm to spark store renovations on key blocks," he said.

Richard D. Parsons, UMEZDC Chair, agreed: "The UMEZ Board of Directors is proud to put our stamp of approval on projects that will boost the business climate in Upper Manhattan, creating new jobs and retaining existing jobs for local residents."

Contact UMEZ at (212) 932-1902.

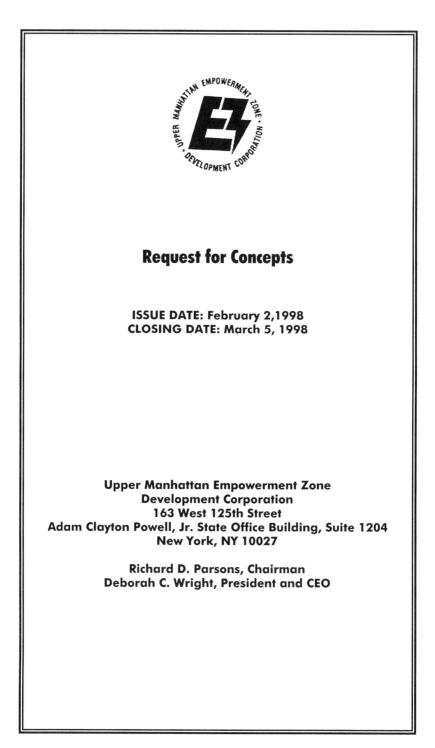

Request for Concepts

ISSUE DATE: February 2,1998
CLOSING DATE: March 5, 1998

Upper Manhattan Empowerment Zone
Development Corporation
163 West 125th Street
Adam Clayton Powell, Jr. State Office Building, Suite 1204
New York, NY 10027

Richard D. Parsons, Chairman
Deborah C. Wright, President and CEO

SUMMARY PAGE
REQUEST FOR CONCEPTS

The Upper Manhattan Empowerment Zone Development Corporation ("UMEZ") requests concepts from the community and other interested parties to develop new and existing businesses and services in target and other industries for Fiscal Year 1998 ("FY 1998") ending June 30, 1999. The Request for Concepts ("RFC") is a two part process. Part One requires submission of an application and a two page concept paper. Part Two requires submission of a complete business plan by selected applicants whose concepts demonstrate the most potential for meeting the UMEZ investment strategy and criteria, the basis upon which funding recommendations will be made. Business plans should be submitted only at the invitation of UMEZ. Such an invitation to complete Part Two does not guarantee funding.

APPLICATION PICK-UP
The RFC provides a detailed description of the process requirements and submissions procedures. Interested parties who wish to request funding may obtain the RFC by calling the UMEZ office at (212) 932-1902 and requesting the RFC or in person between the hours of 9:00 am and 5:30 pm, Monday through Friday, beginning Monday, February 2, 1998.

Upper Manhattan Empowerment Zone
Development Corporation
Adam Clayton Powell, Jr. State Office Building, Suite 1204
163 West 125th Street,
between Adam Clayton Powell Blvd. and Lenox Avenue
New York, NY 10027

On March 2,1998, the UMEZ will move its offices to 290 Lenox Avenue, at 125th Street. After this date, RFCs will be available-at the new location. All RFC responses should then also be submitted to that location.

CLOSING DATE

The deadline for submission of 5 Copies of the completed application and concept paper under this RFC is Thursday, March 5, 1998, at 3:00 pm. No late applications or concepts will be accepted, except if postmarked at least 2 business days prior to deadline or if via Express Mail at least one business day prior to deadline.

TARGET INDUSTRIES

As described in the RFC, priority will be given to concepts in the following target industries:

■ Entertainment/Tourism: includes, but not limited to: expansion of existing and creation of new restaurants, amusement/recreational facilities museums, gift and novelty shops featuring community products, taxi and shuttle services, bed & breakfasts, hotels, tourist centers tour guide books, maps, signage parking, and other general tourism initiatives.

■ Retail: includes, but not limited to apparel/accessories, book stores, record/tape stores, food stores, general merchandise, and furniture/home furnishings. Focus is on growth and upgrading local services and amenities.

Applicants should note that UMEZ may review concepts that are not in our target industries However, such projects may not be reviewed until after completion of review in our priority industries.

SUBMISSION PROCESS

This RFC is a two part process. Part One is the submission of an application and two page concept paper. Part Two requires submission of a complete business plan by selected applicants whose concepts demonstrate the most potential for meeting the UMEZ investment strategy and criteria, the basis upon which funding recommendations will be made. Business plans should be submitted only at the invitation of UMEZ Such an invitation to complete Part Two does not guarantee funding. Upon review, if any items are missing and/or incomplete, UMEZ, at its discretion, may notify the applicant to provide such items. Failure to provide complete information in a timely fashion could result in rejection of the application. Submission of concept papers shall be deemed to be permission by the applicant for UMEZ to make such inquiries concerning the applicant as deemed necessary. Responses will be reviewed by a committee of the UMEZ Board of Directors All material submitted by applicants shall become the property of UMEZ. Disbursement of funds will not occur until applicants are approved by the UMEZ Board and the New York Empowerment Zone Corporation Board and all funding agreements are properly executed.

PRE-SUBMISSION CONFERENCE

A pre-submission conference with UMEZ staff, where interested parties can ask questions regarding this RFC, will be held on Friday, February 20, 1998, at 3:00 pm at Julia De Burgos Latino Cultural Center, 1680 Lexington Avenue at East 106th Street.

Questions for the pre-submission conference should be submitted in writing by mail or fax in advance to Rhona Gibson, Director of New Business Development, UMEZDC, 163 West 125th Street, Suite 1204, New York, N.Y. 10027, fax number (212) 932-1669.

L. Record Retention

The Contractor, during the course of the contract resulting from the RFC and for a period of six (6) years following its termination, or final payment thereunder, whichever occurs later, agrees to maintain and make available for audit by duly authorized representative of UMEZ, all financial records or documentation thereunder.

M. Reporting

Contractors must prepare and submit regular progress and financial reports, comprehensive final reports on a yet to be determined schedule and shall be required to cooperate with UMEZ, its designated outside evaluator, and City, State and/or Federal agencies in conducting evaluation activities, and audit of program financial records. In addition, upon contract completion, contractors must submit a final report that summarizes and evaluates the activities of the entire project.

N. Compliance With Laws

All proposed programs shall conform to, and be subject to, the provision of all applicable laws, regulations and ordinances of all Federal, State, and City authorities having jurisdiction, as the same may be amended from time to time.

O. Vendex

The contract awards shall be subject to completion of City, State, and Federal contract monitoring And background investigation procedures such as a New York City VENDEX Questionnaire. Only organizations recommended for funding by the UMEZ will be subject to these procedures.

Newcomers to 125th Street like Duane Reade, Rite Aid and Blockbuster Video are now found among such landmarks as Theresa Towers (center) and the National Black Theater (detail at right).

Retailers Have Harlem on Their Mind

Harlem U.S.A. With 275,000 square feet, would include a Disney store, Gap, nine screen Cineplex Odeo Theater and ice skating rink.

STATE OF TENNESSEE
HUMAN RIGHTS COMMISSION
CENTRAL OFFICE
Cornerstone Square Building, Suite 400
530 Church Street
Nashville, Tennessee 37243-0745
Phone 615/741-5825

February 18, 1998

Ms. Dorothy Hughes, Proprietor
Harlem Office Supplies
121 West 125th St.
NY, NY 10027

Dear Ms. Hughes:

It was great meeting you at the New York State Association of Black
and Puerto Rican Legislators, Inc. weekend in Albany. I thought it
was a stimulating meeting and found the sessions most informative.
One of the things I really enjoyed was the opportunity to meet you
during my Title VI class on Saturday. Besides my being the state
director for Title VI in Tennessee, I am also a partner in a consulting
firm, Public Policy Matters, LLC.

We are seeking to expand awareness of Title VI of the 1964 Civil Rights
Act. Title VI is the single most powerful weapon to impact public
expenditures supporting economic development. The enforcement of
Title VI of Civil Rights Act of 1964 and its impact on public policy has
national implications. African-American business and its community
leaders have not been involved in a substantial way with the formula-
tion of public policy to advance its economic interests. The idea is to
exert influence over public spending and participation so that the
majority private sector cannot get public money without input from

the African-American community. Title VI of the Civil Rights Act of 1964 is our standing invitation to take a proactive posture with respect to public policy at the state and local government levels. It is important to raise the level of awareness of African Americans to understand the national and local implications of Title VI so as to improve the economic and social conditions in their communities.

I enclosed some information

■ Comptroller of the Treasury - January 1994 report—*"Tennessee State Agencies and Title VI of the 1964 Civil Rights Act"*— I was the senior research analyst on this study Since the release of the report in January 1994, we have sent out approximately 15,000 copies. This is the blue report, everyone was asking for at the meeting.

■ Public Policy Matters Brochure

■ Afro-Gazette magazine with us on the front cover

If you have any questions, I can be reached at (615) 532-5027 from 8:00 a.m. to 5:00 p.m. and at (615) 354-0281 after 5:30 and at my voice mail pager 615-402-9488

Sincerely,

Kimberly J. Bandy
Title VI Program Director

The New New York Beacon, May 6-May 12, 1999

Multi-Million Dollar Lawsuit Against Empowerment Zone

Dorothy Pitman Hughes, the owner of Harlem Office Supply Inc., previously located at 121 West 125th Street in Harlem, says she has retained a law firm to investigate what appears to be a pattern of "economic cleansing" of African-American businesses on the busiest shopping strip in Harlem by the Harlem centered Empowerment Zone.

Hughes, one of the few black businesswomen store owners left on 125th Street, claims to have identified a concerted and consistent program by the Upper Manhattan Empowerment Zone to drive out local businesses in favor of the chains and non-local entrepreneurs who have been ignoring Harlem for most of the century.

Hughes says, local businesses fail for want of capital even as the Upper Manhattan Empowerment Zone distributes hundreds of thousands of dollars of public money to established business people like actor Robert DiNiro, who are easily able to obtain the financing local business people simply cannot obtain.

She has instructed her lawyers, Johnston & Sellers, LLP, to investigate the pattern of financing by the Upper Manhattan Empowerment Zone since its inception. She states that "this program, designed to trigger a new Harlem renaissance has served instead, to kill off the businesses which have served Harlem through its darkest economic days."

Hughes further stated that the company, a stationary and office supply business, had been located for eight of eighteen years in the same location and now her rent was raised to $7,500 from $4,221. "If it wasn't for the support of the community and the 5,000 shareholders, who, by the way are voters, I would be out of business. The City of New York, who is my landlord, in collusion with the Upper Manhattan Empowerment Zone leaders, basically said to me, pay the $7,500 or get out." With her shareholders support, she was able to find another location at 6 East 125th Street.

Hughes says she believes, "The reason that I am being treated this way is because the Upper Manhattan Empowerment Zone may be trying to attract a large store like Staples and my local community business is an obstacle."

A fierce fighter for the rights of small minority owned business. Hughes says she is knowledgeable of the Upper Manhattan Empowerment Zone and how it operates because she was the only Black female business owner on the Economic Development Committee when the Empowerment Zone was being formed.

She had seen a number of Black businesses suffer as a result of the Upper Manhattan Empowerment Zone, because some of them, anticipating some financial assistance from the Empowerment Zone, went out on a limb upgrading and expanding their businesses."

When the economic development assistance didn't come through, she observed, "many of them were Caught between a rock and a hard place."

Furthermore, Hughes says, "I am sure that my treatment and what has happened to other Black businesses in Harlem is in violation of a number of federal and state law," she concluded.

Hughes will release a statement of specific patterns of discrimination she claims at a meeting on Thursday, May 6th, 10:00 a.m. at the now empty Harlem Office Supply store, 121 West 125th Street, just yards away from Blockbusters at Starbucks' new 125th street address.

When the media questioned H.O.S., Inc.'s exclusion, they were told that I, Dorothy P, Hughes, was not a good businesswoman. I'd like to know what they call a businesswoman who has survived for seventeen years in *this* climate! When I asked how that was determined I was told that it was determined by me because I owe $23,000 in taxes and was late in paying rent to the city. My reply: The New York and New Jersey Tax Amnesty laws are not written for me, but rather for American business owners who owe *millions* of dollars in taxes. And I am not by any stretch the only one in New York who has been late in paying their rent but I have been one of the only ones on 125th Street to be charged a substantially higher rent because of gender and race.

Empowerment Zones were legislated to assist people like myself who have been systematically left out of the economic mainstream. I have survived as a businesswoman while working to support other Harlem business owners, at the same time working to win Empowerment Zone funding for Harlem, only to be denied its help *because* I needed it.

I was even excluded from the list of invited business owners to the EZ meetings. When they held a meeting at Harlem's Apollo Theatre, attended by Vice-President Al Gore and Andrew Cuomo (Secretary of the U.S. Dept. of Housing & Urban Development) I was not one of the invitees but I went anyway. I was blocked from entering, and told that I had not been cleared for the meeting. I asked, "who does the clearing?", and was finally allowed in. Just as I made promises to be a great disturbance, the caterer of the event put a pan of food in my hands saying, "Dorothy, please carry this in for me." So, instead of entering the EZ meeting as an entrepreneur—being the only black female in the State of New York to own this type of business, I entered the meeting as a servant—relegated to that position by persons of my own race and gender. But as we already learned from our Webster's description, we encounter classism in gentrification.

Dorothy Pitman Hughes thanks City Council President Ruth Messinger for participating in her Sojourner Bed and Breakfast Fundraiser at Avery Fisher Hall in Manhattan.

I continued to point to that which was destroying black businesses' ability to participate in business in our community. Most often I was told, "The reason you all don't get contracts is that blacks don't want to do the paper work that's required." Of course this is not the case. What I did find to be true is that I was caught up in a no-win situation. A cycle of seeing more and more of the people whose opportunities I have fought for—to go to colleges and universities and to be elected into positions of power—turning their backs on the community. A cycle of people with what are called "good jobs" preferring to spend their own money outside the community black owned businesses. And of looking to corporate America for what little they can get *now*, while the getting's good, rather than using their power to build against the threat of decimation which looms over our community's future.

When I began to look at my business—office supplies and furniture, computers, computer hardware and software, stationery, business cards, rubber stamps, etc.—I saw that one month of office supply spending from the agency in charge of planning for the EZ could have sent my business to a new level.

Here is something I read recently in the "EZ Journal":

> *"The spirit we bring to our work will make the difference. We must be committed to the pursuit of opportunity for all Americans and we must be committed to a new kind of government, not to solve all our problems for us but to give our people the tools they need to make the most of their own lives."*
>
> *President William Clinton*
> *State of the Union Address*
> *February 4, 1997*

> *"We need to create a climate where families can flourish and hope can blossom."*
>
> *Vice President Al Gore*
> *Budget Announcement*
> *February 6, 1997*

It is clear that the "spirit" of the legislation alluded to by President Clinton is lost on the EZ ambassadors.

The EZ funding designates that $100 Million each be contributed by the federal, state and city governments. The city is contributing much of its share through its city-owned real estate; which it is selling through a leveraging process. Great, new ownership in

Harlem. Finally, the beautiful brownstones and buildings in Harlem which we've seen boarded up for years while people lived on the street will come back to life. But who will end up owning these buildings? And who will populate them?

There is a move to push people out of inner cities as the exodus of white upper and middle-class America from the suburbs back into the cities picks up steam. Large public housing structures are coming down all over the country (as on Chicago's lakefront and in the heart of Harlem) and more moderate housing is going up. We must be aware when assessing these new moves which are being billed as "bettering" the housing conditions for the poor, that these properties are now considered prime real estate; and we must consider where the former residents will go and what lies ahead for them there.

The EZ plan calls for a ten year "demonstration" that through its funding, the EZ communities can sustain the economic and social empowerment of their people. What happens after ten years if the plan fails? We go back to the government stance that was emerging in the language and legislation of its officials in the 80's and early 90's—that we simply must accept a permanent underclass (due, presumably to the inherent inability of certain segments of society to build and sustain economic parity with mainstream America) which no amount of money "thrown at them" will help.

Some are convinced that the current EZ plans of empowering large corporations to provide low paying jobs for our residents will bring economic empowerment to a community which has historically been discriminated against. While I support the original plan (as I understood it from the Economic Empowerment Planning Committee on which I served for eleven months) to build an economic base through black business, I do not believe that we will economically empower enough African-Americans through this philosophy of sacrificing African-American business for jobs.

To create a strong foundation for spring-boarding economic empowerment in the 21st century, making sure that African-American people have what President Clinton and the Harlem community called for to take us through the next millennium, we must look to the community itself—to its resources and creativity, to the power and momentum of its own desire to survive and flourish.

Much of what little advancement there has been in Harlem over the past thirty years has resulted from the efforts of African-American business owners who have managed to stay in business despite the difficulties placed before us.

Although others choose to trivialize the importance of our endeavors, African-American entrepreneurs in Harlem, collectively, provide jobs for hundreds of people who live in our community.

Small business employment of Harlem residents is second only to government jobs. We keep families out of the welfare system. We train youngsters in skills that the educational system of this city leaves lacking—skills that they cannot go "downtown" to learn at the expense of the employers there. We provide part-time jobs for students; and there have been many young men and women saved from "street life" because black business owners took the time and gave them the opportunity to earn an honest dollar.

Many may not want to concern themselves with the reality of "street life" when addressing economic development. But doesn't that stance presuppose that there is simply a certain percentage of the population who are, and will continue to be, criminals and drug-abusers? The numbers don't pan out. Even if you are willing to say that in all populations there will be that element of people who are "lost causes", you must admit that we as a community have many more than our share of this "element" unless you are willing to believe that more of us are genetically or culturally predisposed to this lifestyle.

Black business' first-hand knowledge of Harlem's problems enhances our ability to operate our businesses with consideration of the specific needs of our employees. Parents can work with the flexibility that allows them to leave for a few moments to see their children safely home from school. We can relate to their need to bring their children to work and to take time off when they have problems with childcare or when their children are ill. We know the value of a few extra hours of work for them. We do what is needed to help them. Ultimately, the community will not reach any healthy level of economic security without the involvement of African-American business owners who understand the intricacies of the role that community-minded economics must play in any revitalization of Harlem. The community cannot benefit from their acumen without specific EZ attention to the severe hardships experienced by these business owners, whose unique experience cannot be addressed through generalities.

Further, in areas so heavily populated by female-headed households, there is unlimited potential for positive change through the economic empowerment of African-American women. We are always in the process of training and educating our employees, our children and ourselves in those skills that are necessary for economic and social advancement. Any increase in our ability to further this process can only result in progressive change for the entire community.

African-American business owners in Harlem have always supported the charitable organizations of this community. We give our time, goods and money. When our politicians need us, we organize fund-raisers and help them campaign for votes.

Therefore, I urge Harlem business owners to make a public call for immediate provisions to be given the financial support that our votes and tax dollars entitle us to. We can help Harlem to become socially and economically sound in ways no one else can.

Harlem business owners must demand an end to our exclusion from the decision making process which governs the economics of our community. We must seek the discontinuation of policies which deny us access to loans and government funds to lock us out of contracts and the bidding process. For the survival of our businesses, and ultimately the community's survival, we must demand an immediate change in policies which result in exorbitant rents, which in some cases are higher for us than for new businesses coming into the area.

For two years, I had represented small African-American business owners as a member of the Economic Development Committee working to help bring about the designation of an Economic Empowerment Zone in Harlem. We believed at the time that we would be the focus for empowerment and that others would come to co-exist with us to create a mix and empower the whole community.

We African-American business owners now feel that we have been used, and that our efforts to empower the community may actually have resulted in accomplishing the gentrification of Harlem, at which attempts have been made for the past 30 years.

Three hundred million dollars have been assigned to this area under the pretext of empowering the residents and businesses in the neighborhood, who have been starved by capital redlining and other discriminatory practices for decades. It now appears that you have to be a large, primarily white-owned business to have access to Empowerment Zone money. It is these large businesses that are now negotiating to come into the area to take advantage of the low-interest loans and tax breaks, while long established local businesses are being denied.

These large businesses may promise to provide employment for residents, but without ownership there is ultimately no empowerment. We smaller, community-starved businesses who have served the community and struggled to keep afloat all these years will be forced to close, while the incoming businesses will benefit. Was this the purpose of the Empowerment Zone?

In our own case, we are aware that efforts are being made to induce the national retail office supply chain into Harlem. If this happens, it will certainly crush Harlem Office supply to death. Thus, we would actually have been better served if the three hundred million dollars had never been given, because it is being used to put black businesses out of business and cause our economic re-enslavement as was written in an article by Michael Grunwald.

> NEW YORK – *Starbucks will hold its grand opening in Harlem Wednesday, bringing its yuppie coffee to America's best-known ghetto. A few blocks east on 125th Street, there was a ribbon cutting last week at a new Pathmark, the first supermarket in a neighborhood with nearly the population of the District. A few blocks west, developers are building Harlem's first mall, featuring the Disney store, HMV Records and a nine-screen movie theater.*
>
> *It may be too soon to call this a second Harlem renaissance, but after decades of decay, the emergence of $3.80 mocha frappuccinos and national chain mega-stores on Harlem's main drag are not the only signs that this one-time cultural and spiritual hub is on the upswing.*

Crime is plummeting. Rents are skyrocketing. Upscale families are restoring elegant brownstones, and not just in the black bourgeois district called "Strivers Row". – A government "empowerment zone" is pumping $550 million into the area. Officials say Harlem has even surpassed the Empire State Building as New York's No. 1 destination for foreign tourists.

Harlem is certainly getting a boost from the prolonged economic boom that has swept the rest of New York and America, but even that spillover effect is a sign of progress. For years, inner-city slums such as Harlem have inhabited a kind of economic vacuum, isolated from the business cycle, deteriorating no matter what. Just a 20-minute subway ride from the euphoria of Wall Street, Harlem finally seems to be rejoining the national economy, and residents hope it finally shed its roll-up-the-windows reputation.

—Michael Grunwald, *Washington Post* Staff Writer

In this article, it was mentioned that Harlem has plenty of critics unhappy with the pace and color of progress. Activists grumble that most of the major Harlem projects are benefitting the white developer rather than local entrepreneurs. And, some critics warn that the new retail projects and gentrification will not solve Harlem's most serious problem.

One well-known resident said, "I'm glad these companies have discovered that poor people want to spend money. What they really need are places to make money, but I just don't think a new mall is going to solve the pathologies here."

The zone's early focus on retail is no accident. One earlier study found that more than 60 per cent of Harlem's money is spent outside the neighborhood and national companies are beginning to sense an untapped market with urban minorities. The president of one large corporation that is moving in told someone, "There's just an unbelievable opportunity here, opportunity with a capital 'O'. I can't believe this. I've got an area the size of Atlanta, and I've got no competition, whatsoever. Think about that."

In fact, the president of that large company will have at least some competition; and therein lies one of the perils for Harlem's future. Some small business owners are angry because they think the Empowerment Zone is providing capital to white corporations while stiffing homegrown black business. Community businesses have been left out from day one.

One local Harlem politician noted that, "Gentrification is two-edged sword. I'm glad to see a mall coming to Harlem, but that's not community investment; that's not building a future."

Many years ago, a black woman proved that "The American Dream" could become a reality for black people. Madame C.J. Walker bears the distinction of having become one of America's first self-made millionaires. It was her money that helped to finance the great era in this city's history known as the "Harlem Renaissance". Today, there are many African-American entrepreneurs in this area with the business savvy and the desire to take this community to even greater heights. Our children may read of Madame Walker as a historical role model but they need more than a distant vision of success. They need empowerment in the here and now. They need to be able to look to the future and be secure in the present. Harlem, a community which has historically represented black self-determination, may soon become the model for gentrification and the establishment of a permanent underclass in America. I don't want that to be our legacy to our children, and I'm sure you don't either.

It has become necessary to find a way to revise our way of thinking and spending so that our money will work to our advantage. We must move from "sharecropping" to "shareholding". As shareholders in our own businesses, we will find our best chance for our economic empowerment and our communities' survival.

Dorothy Pitman Hughes attends a party to celebrate South Africa's Freedom.

Chapter Eight
Patterns of Exclusion

(Sojourner Bed & Breakfast)

In 1989 I was approved for a loan from the Small Business Administration (SBA) to assist in construction work on a brownstone I purchased for the purpose of opening a Bed & Breakfast at 2007 Fifth Avenue in Harlem. I was also given support from some friends, such as Alice Walker and Gloria Steinem which, because of their celebrity status, became interesting news for newspapers. Three weeks later, I was denied the already approved loan from the SBA. The denial was based on an erroneous report in a newspaper that my operation would be based on a "time-sharing" concept. Rather, I had taken a contribution from Alice Walker and was discussing that in order to raise additional funds for the completion of the B&B, I was considering having people "buy" reservations for the rooms to use in the future, any time they wanted, after the B&B was up and running. The following letters illustrate the confusion:

July 18, 1989   FD:RG

Business Loan Center, Inc.
79 Madison Avenue, Suite 800
New York, NY 10016
Attn: Mr. Donald Krauss

Re: Sojourner Bed & Breakfast
GP 342132-30-03 NY

Dear Mr. Krause:

Pursuant to our telephone conversation which took place earlier today, please be advised that questions regarding the eligibility of the above referenced applicant for SBA related financial assistance remain unanswered. You have indicated that it is the intentions of Business Loan center, Inc. to close this loan on July 19, 1989. This letter is to be considered a formal notice to the Business Loan center, Inc. that this loan not close until the eligibility issue has been addressed to this Agency's satisfaction.

You are requested to furnish additional information as to whether or not Mrs. Hughes bed and breakfast concept represents a real estate offering under General Business Law Statute 352e. If so, were the proper documents filed with the appropriate governmental agencies which control these matters? If not, why weren't they filed? You are also requested to furnish more information on the "Time Sharing" concept under which Mrs. Hughes indicated her business would operate including how many slots had she already sold as well as how many she was intending on selling? You are further requested to indicate whether or not Business Loan Center, Inc. took the extra monies realized from these transactions into consideration in the original loan proposal?

Upon receipt and review of the requested information, you will be advised as to the outcome.

                              Very truly yours,

                              Ronald Goldstein, Loan Officer

Small Business Access to Money

July 19, 1989

Dorothy P. Hughes
2007 5th Avenue
New York, New York

Re: SBA Loan application

Dear Ms. Hughes

This letter is intended to clarify the confusion surrounding the approval of your SBA loan application. While your application was being reviewed by the SBA, a newspaper article came out indicating that the proposed bed & breakfast would be involved in a "Time Sharing" concept. This raised questions regarding the eligibility of the business for SBA related financial assistance. To date, these questions have not been answered to the satisfaction of the SBA. Until this has been resolved, the guaranty of the SBA is NOT in effect.

Enclosed is a formal notice from the SBA regarding this matter. Please have your attorney furnish the proper documentation to be forwarded to the SBA.

Once the issue of eligibility has been resolved, we can proceed with satisfying the terms and conditions necessary to close this loan.

If you have any questions, please call me.

Very truly yours,

Bruce Agnew

Dorothy Pitman Hughes celebrates her 60th birthday with longtime friend Gloria Steinem at the Cotton Club.

Gloria Steinem and I wrote affidavits, got them notarized and took them, through the pouring rain, down to the SBA Loan Center, along with the correction from the news reporter; but when I arrived, I was still black and female with a great idea for a business in Harlem. I was still denied the loan.

I had put the word out. Everyone was talking about my project. There was support from my friends, the entertainment community and from corporations who care about people like me. After much effort to get assistance; pointing out the exclusion of my proposals to the leaders of Harlem and the City of New York, I was called for an interview on The Bill Cosby Show on why I wanted to put a Bed & Breakfast in Harlem. I pointed out the need for such an operation and facts about the gentrification of Harlem and talked about the fact that my building was in a historic area. Shortly after the show, I received a letter of support from the New York Landmark Conservancy. This was encouraging, but I was still being denied assistance.

Determined to open a B&B in Harlem, I appealed to the social consciousness of Michel Roux, then president of Absolut Vodka. Absolut committed to helping us with two evenings of fund-raising at Lincoln Center and the Cotton Club. Cotton Club owner, John Beatty, Gloria Steinem and many, many other friends and acquaintances came out in support. We partied with Arthur Prysock and other entertainers, and funds were raised to start the renovations of the B&B site. We were able to bring this old brownstone, which had been vacant for twelve years, to a point where new plumbing was being installed. Now we were at the phase where we would update the electrical circuits.

We put out a call to any black, non-profit organization who might assist us with building plans and the disbursement of the funds we had raised for a good fee. Two major black organizations promised to take on the assignment; but as I would not give those organizations control over my building and project, they refused to accept the funds and the responsibility to assist us.

I was in shock when one of Harlem's leading news reporters came to my office, handed me a magazine article, and said, "Dorothy, I thought you should see this. I'm sorry they keep doing this to you." Here is the article, which was in *Crain's New York Business* two years after I discussed my plans with HUDC (Harlem Urban Development Corp.)

Five Groups Receive Development Grants

Five New York City community groups have received a total of $231,000 I grants from New York state for economic development projects.

The Urban Development Corp. Awarded the money to groups in the Bronx and Manhattan under the UDC's urban and community development program.

The groups are Banana Kelly Community Improvement Association, which received $40,000 to study building a commercial structure for retail use on a city-owned piece of land in the South Bronx.

Bathgate Industrial Park's Local Development Corp. Will get $41,000 to study the rehabilitation of a four-story building owned by the city. The structure would be used as an incubator for small businesses.

Also in the Bronx, New Directions in Community Revitalization received $50,000 to study turning a city-owned building into commercial space that would also be used for child care.

In Manhattan, Harlem Restoration Corp. Got $50,000 to study rehabilitation of a 140,000-square-foot building into a commercial/industrial facility that would house a small-business incubator.

Manhattan Borough Development Corp. Got $50,000 to study creating a bed-and-breakfast hotel in Harlem that is tentatively dubbed Harlem Renaissance Inn.

The hotel would be located in central Harlem above a restaurant and club.

New
York
Landmarks
Conservancy   April 25, 1994

Ms. Dorothy Pitman Hughes
609 West 138th Street
New York, New York 10031

Re: Sojourner Bed &
Breakfast, 2007 Fifth
Avenue, Manhattan

Dear Dorothy:

As you know, the new York Landmarks Conservancy is a private, not-for-profit organization that is dedicated to the preservation of landmark quality buildings and neighborhoods throughout the City of New York. The Mount Morris Park area, which includes 2007 Fifth Avenue, is one of the communities to which we have targeted our financials and technical resources; our organization has several projects within the Mount Morris Park Historic District and hopes to assist with as many others as possible.

We believe that the proposed use of 2007 Fifth Avenue as the Sojourner Bed & Breakfast will make an important contribution to this thriving area. The Conservancy would be pleased to extend its redevelopment resources to the endeavor in the forms of providing a) project management assistance and b) a low-interest (3%) loan of $100,000 from the NYC Historic Properties Fund, subject to various customary terms and conditions being met.

We stand ready to help you bring this enterprise to fruition.

Sincerely,

Karen Ansis
Manager
NYC Historic Properties Fund

121

Dismayed, but undeterred, some of my good friends, who included Sam Peabody, Carol Jenkins, Gloria Steinem and Mark Hampton, co-hosted a fund-raising evening at the National Black Theatre for the B&B, In organizing the function, we managed to keep our monies in the Harlem community by utilizing the National Black Theatre's hall, which was decorated with artwork from Afri-works and having Harlem's own Cotton Club cater the affair. We hired party planners from the community, and a 16-piece orchestra from Harlem's Wells Restaurant.

Next we had a celebrity auction at the Cotton Club. Among the donors were Eddie Murphy, Bill Cosby, Percy Sutton and Gloria Steinem. The funds raised went to the electrical wiring work and some restorations of the interior of the building.

By this time the work was almost complete, so I was encouraged to submit my proposal to our new Upper Manhattan Empowerment Zone. We all just *knew* that this was the place to take this wonderful idea that already had the interest and support of so many.

The Sojourner Bed & Breakfast Proposal, as submitted to the Upper Manhattan Empowerment Zone Committee in 1996:

SOJOURNER BED & BREAKFAST
2007 FIFTH AVENUE, HARLEM N.Y. 10035

The Concept

IN KEEPING WITH THE STRENGTH OF SPIRIT, tenacity and vision that made Sojourner Truth a reigning force in African-American history, Dorothy Pitman Hughes' *Sojourner Bed and Breakfast* is a progressive endeavor combining entrepreneurship, ambassadorship, cultural preservation and social revitalization of a community.

A true renaissance is taking root in the Harlem community. Restoration and construction projects are in progress throughout the area. The people are joining together to create investment partnerships, action committees and social forums. The community is renewing and preparing itself to reclaim its position as a vital and progressive arena for the arts, politics and social movements.

Since there are no other facilities of its kind in the area, *Sojourner Bed and Breakfast* is designed to be an integral part of what this renaissance is all about.

As more and more tourists, performance artists, politicians and dignitaries return to Harlem for entertainment, cultural affairs and political or business functions, the Bed and Breakfast will service the needs of those requiring lodgings for one or several nights. There will even be a presidential suite reserved for government leaders who will soon find themselves compelled to return to this community as more and more barriers which inhibited their presence before are destroyed.

Befitting its Fifth Avenue location, the building itself will be an upscale facility designed for comfort, understated elegance and refinement by world renowned decorators Peter Marino and Mark Hampton, both of whom have committed themselves to this project through Samuel P. Peabody. Home-away-from-home ambiance will be enhanced by the waking of guests to aromas of baking breads, fresh-brewed coffees, and preparation of hearty domestic and international dishes for guests' consumption. The atrium will be available for dining, private conferences and small receptions.

To preserve and promote the history and culture of African-Americans, each room will be named in honor of an historical individual. There will be an abundance of literature on the African American Experience, and literature and information to encourage guests to visit the many historical sights within Harlem. Tours will be arranged for guests upon request.

Herein lies the concept for *Sojourner Bed and Breakfast*: an entrepreneurial venture designed to achieve financial success through the promotion of community culture and good will, while servicing the needs of an increasing customer market. It is a viable concept that has the potential of making *Sojourner Bed and Breakfast* a central point for the exchange of ideas and viewpoints, due to the varied backgrounds of individuals for which it is suitable.

THE THEME

Because of the rich history of Harlem, tourists as well as New Yorkers are interested in knowing what Harlem is all about. This interest gives us an opportunity to present a positive image.

Certainly one way for people to get to know each other is a visit in the home. Sojourner offers this to the community. Since there are only eight (8) rental rooms we cannot house even a small busload. Therefore, the idea of the Bed and Breakfast society of Harlem was born. For a small yearly fee the Bed and Breakfast Society will register additional owners in the area who have beautiful rooms which would conform to the Society's by-laws and regulations.

The cleaning up before and after would be the society's responsibility as well as all personal service and amenities.

SOJOURNER BED & BREAKFAST

2007 FIFTH AVENUE, HARLEM N.Y. 10035

The Motif

THERE WILL BE EIGHT ELEGANTLY DECORATED ROOMS, which will each be named in honor of an historical figure. Most of the original details of the building will be preserved. Each room will have its own bathroom, air conditioner, and separate heating controls. Restoration of fireplaces, wood floors, stairs, banisters and moldings will contribute to the ambiance of the setting. For dining and meeting comfort, a beautiful atrium will be added to the rear of the building. There will be ample information in each room about Harlem's sights of interest, including maps, souvenirs, tickets to special events and postcards. There will also be an abundance of literature about African American history.

Tours will be arranged upon request. The overall motif will create an atmosphere of refined comfort. The specific décor of each room will be decided with the expert assistance of Peter Marino and Mark Hampton, to reflect its individual warmth and beauty through color, fabric and choice of furnishings.

SOJOURNER BED & BREAKFAST
2007 FIFTH AVENUE, HARLEM N.Y. 10035

Marketing

SELLING POINTS

- Reasonable fees.
- Delicious cuisine.
- Elegant décor.
- Ideal Fifth Avenue locale.
- Close proximity to many other establishments such as the Schomburg Center, Apollo Theatre, Abyssinian Baptist Church, Grant's Tomb, The Body Shop, Ben & Jerry's, the National Black Theatre, and Sylvia's Restaurant.

STRATEGY

- Attract a varied clientèle ranging from international dignitaries to locals celebrating special occasions.
- Promote the Renaissance and its positive changes.
- Reflect the upscale ambiance that is unique to New York's Fifth Avenue.
- Maintain an image of the "in" place to stay while visiting New York.

MARKETING VEHICLES

- Tri-State Directory and newspaper ads.
- New York Visitors and Convention Bureau.
- Tour Companies, including private bus and limousine services.
- Travel Agencies, specializing in bookings from European and Asian countries, political personages and/or small tour groups.

The proposal was funded, but not to me. I was brought at least fifteen copies of this article by concerned neighbors and people of the Harlem community. (Note the address of the new B&B).

BRISC BRIEFS

News from the Business Resource & Investment Service Center   Summer 1998

BRISC Loans Support Restaurant, Retail and Bed & Breakfast Businesses

BRISC ended fiscal year 1998 with loans to four local businesses. Through BRISC, Upper Manhattan businesses accessed over $1.5 million in capital to date. Through its Investment Fund, BRISC provided loans that helped create and expand the small businesses described below.

Cafe Largo: $100,000

Located at 3387 Broadway at West 137th Street, Café Largo is a full service restaurant that offers continental as well as Latin American and Italian cuisine. The restaurant, which opened on June 6th near City College, offers both take out and dining services for up to 70 people. Marc Calcano, a lifetime resident of the West Harlem/Washington Heights community, owns the business. The $100,000 BRISC investment was used for leasehold improvements, equipment purchases, inventory and working capital.

Urban Jem Guest House: $50,000

The Urban Jem Guest House, owned by Jane Alex Mendelson, is a four-room bed & breakfast located at 2005 Fifth Avenue. Ms. Mendelson purchased the 1878 brownstone in February 1997 and renovated it to include two studio apartments with a private kitchen and bath and two furnished rooms which share a bathroom and kitchen. The $50,000 BRISC investment will be used for leasehold improvements, working capital expenses and debt consolidation.

St. Mark's Place: $25,000

St. Mark's Place is the recipient of a $25,000 BRISC loan. Located at 2337 Frederick Douglass Boulevard at West 125th Street, St. Mark's has grown from its original location at Mart 125 to its current retail space in only two years. Owner Mark Brantley, a third generation Harlem entrepreneur, initially sold men's clothing; suits, shirts, belts and sportswear. However, after a few samples of women's and children's clothing flew off the rack, he decided to expand his inventory. St. Mark's Place will now carry women and children's sportswear, casual wear and dresses. The BRISC loan will be used to purchase the additional inventory and for store renovations to increase display and storage space.

Sylvia's Creative Novelty: $25,000

Sylvia's Creative Novelty, a start-up owned by Sylvia Lorenzo, is located at 1753 Lexington Avenue at 110th Street. Ms. Lorenzo opened this storefront beneath her apartment earlier this spring. Sylvia's Creative Novelty is a party goods store, offering a wide variety of products for all special occasions, including invitations, cards and helium balloons. In addition, Ms. Lorenzo creates custom handicrafts, wedding and baptism gowns. She also consults clients on the planning of functions such as weddings and sweet sixteens. The BRISC investment will be used for leasehold improvements, equipment purchases and working capital expenses.

Franklin Bonifacio photo

Sylvia's Creative Novelty

Franklin Bonifacio photo

St. Mark's Place
Customers have a greater choice of

Rodney Lopez photo

Urban Jem Guest House
Jane Mendelson is welcoming more

Franklin Bonifacio photo

Cafe Largo
Friends and family celebrate the

Dorothy Pitman Hughes spending time with son-in-law film producer Paul Quinn and daughter Patrice Pitman Quinn at their Hollywood home.

Dorothy's daughters Delethia Marvin and Angela Hughes with her grandson Sean Ridley enjoying each other's company at home in Harlem.

Chapter Nine
Discovering My Strength

> *"Freedom!*
> *A fine word when rightly understood.*
> *What freedom would you have?*
> *What is the freedom of the most free?*
> *To act rightly!"*
>
> *—Goethe*

This chapter is for those of us who have felt like we could not "go home again." As I stand in the kitchen of my brownstone in Harlem this Sunday morning, picking my two bunches of turnips and one bunch of collard greens, having put the meat for this evening's dinner on the stove to boil, it dawns on me that I have never left my home in Charles Junction. Home is with me wherever I travel in space or time. "I am at home," I think, while peeling the roots of the purple topped turnips that were not raised by me but well could have been if I were not involved in raising consciousness at the moment! And I wonder, if I had not known how to raise turnips, chicken, peas or corn, would I have been this confident in my ability to help raise consciousness in my community? Yes, I'm sure I have never left home, and that it was that home which taught me the survival techniques that have led me to this place and time.

I find myself day after day drawing upon the lessons learned at home; as I go about my activities at work in the store, and in the community. It is not difficult for me to understand and talk with children, for instance, because when I was a child, it was a natural thing to give respect and to be given respect in our community. Adults talked with us, played with us, taught us and learned from us.

I came to New York, and to the test of who I am; and how I wish to know myself becomes apparent. I am a whole woman, and as such I wish to know myself as a person who is a good mother, daughter, sister, grandmother, wife, aunt, friend, employer and community activist. I believe that people know me as a person who will try to do what I promise. My word is my bond.

Years ago, the Honorable Percy E. Sutton, whom I respect so much, said to me: "Dorothy, it's so good to know that you still believe in helping the poor out of poverty." I do. And I suppose my strength *comes from* helping others, and hopefully, helping to close the economic gap between African-Americans and others so that we can truly experience our power and strength as a people.

I have worked and studied to gain skills in the areas of research, urban planning, sociology and political science; and one course of learning that was a must for me was Political Analysis of Social Programs. Working with Professor Charles Hamilton when I was a Metropolitan Applied Research Center Fellow helped me see that it is not possible to have political or social power without economic power.

I have dedicated my entire life to being an advocate for the powerless, and have—with the support of many friends and colleagues, and to the dismay of many adversarial forces—achieved much of what I have set out to do. My present exclusion from economic support from the EZ has become the fuel for my attempt to light the fire of ownership and entrepreneurship by African-Americans in the new millennium.

Chapter Ten
We Have the Power

"Where there is no vision the people perish."

Pr. 29:18.

When trying to get past the disappointment of not being accepted as a beneficiary of any support from the Empowerment Zone ambassadors and Board of Directors, something was revealed to me, for which I will always be grateful to God. *We already have the power to make our community whole.* This is what I envision, and will continue to work toward:

1. We will own shares in the businesses of our communities.

2. We will move our dollars from banks that will not give us loans to do business.

3. We will build bridges, from our communities to the spending of black churches; from our communities to the spending of black colleges; from our communities to all service agencies in our communities; and finally, bridges from people to people in our communities.

4. We will own shares in the large corporations that have discovered inner city communities *and our dollars.*

5. We will support the development of black ownership with black entrepreneurial control of businesses instead of black ownership as fronts for white control.

6. Black business will join forces through mutual funds— empowering our communities directly.

Dorothy Pitman Hughes with former U.S. Senator from Illinois, Carol Mosely Braun.

I believe that we must, *and will* see a more confident and self-empowered nation of African-Americans in the early 21st century. We will put aside the disappointment of being denied our "40 acres and a mule" and we will use our consumer power to create black industry. We will *Wake Up and Smell the Dollars!*

Chapter Eleven
"Empowerment" or "Enslavement"?

After all I've seen and been through, Empowerment Zones can still be the answer to our prayers, but all must acknowledge what is happening in each of the legislated EZ's and fix what is wrong.

We must address and oppose the EZ's sponsorship of the failure of black owned businesses for which the legislation was intended. We must address and oppose the present EZ philosophy of creating "jobs" for our children when the current minimum wage in this country is only $5.10 per hour. As new prisons are being built every day, and the new inner-city infrastructures are forming, the stage is being set for our families and our children's families to try to survive in the new millennium on $5.10 per hour; with even fewer opportunities for ownership, and fewer options for economic empowerment.

We are paying for this deadly scenario with our tax dollars, our consumer dollars, and our silence.

The EZ proposal to the federal government points to the racial biases leveraged against the people of Harlem and states that these biases would be eliminated in the communities which obtained EZ status. A couple of examples of the businesses the Upper Manhattan Empowerment Zone is supporting: a project called Harlem USA, which includes Disney, The Gap, Old Navy, and Sony Theatre Complex ($11,200,000); Minton's Playhouse, Robert DeNiro and Drew Nieporent, owners ($400,000).

I'm sure many Harlem residents would like to have a Gap store in the neighborhood but until The Gap benefits our community beyond saving people train fare "downtown," what does The Gap have to do with our community's empowerment? Do we own shares in Disney? Further, how many producers of Disney films, how many Disney executives, how many Disney merchandisers are black, or live in this community? How many of our residents, if "empowered" with $5.10 an hour jobs in these outposts, will *ever* have the opportunity to be Sony executives, and start to reap the benefits of having a Sony Theatre Complex in a community which spends millions of dollars each year on entertainment?

Ownership = Power

Decide what "empowerment" means to you when assessing the achievements of the Empowerment Zone. To my mind, "Empowerment" through the EZ program would mean:

▼ Nurturing both the development of large-scale commercial ventures and small retail businesses in a way that they co-exist without conflict. This would enable new, large chains to become part of the community without destroying the existing small businesses and all that they offer the community.

▼ Access, for small minority-owned businesses, to capital, tax incentive programs and loans (considered too expensive for the banking community to process) to create new minority-owned businesses and assist existing businesses to expand through a variety of financial vehicles: Harlem's own community development bank, venture capital, and other investment tools.

▼ Maximized support and the drawing in of the ethnic and cultural diversity and experience of the people of the community, who are primarily African-American, Puerto Rican and Dominican.

▼ Economic development projects viewed with the goal of economic benefits accruing to the community and its residents.

▼ Training and job opportunities co-existing with all economic development efforts, from housing to the creation and/or retention of business in the community.

▼ Harlem's minority corporations creating joint ventures to enable them to obtain larger percentages of business in a given industry.

▼ A new design of business ownership in which employees and the community at large are stockholders in the business ventures developed.

▼ Financing and development insuring that businesses operating within the Empowerment Zone pay adequate benefits to employees.

You *are* being affected by the EZ legislation, you simply must assess what end of the bargain you're coming out on. If you live in or near one of the newly legislated EZ's, begin to list the changes and see if they affect you in a positive way (other than not having to go all the way "downtown" to rent movies at Blockbuster). Does the Empowerment Zone economically empower you? If it does, share with your neighbor how he or she can benefit. Teach them to gain support from it. If it does not economically empower you, join with others and form a group of "EZ Warriors" and confront the Board of Directors at your EZ.

And if you have an opportunity to invest in your community by buying stock, or simply choosing to spend your money in community businesses, do it. *Where we spend our money is where we give our power!* **Wake up and smell the dollars!**

Dorothy Pitman Hughes is greeted by Reverend Jesse Jackson at his fund raising party for the Rainbow Coalition, which took place on Wall Street's trading floor in 1999.

Chapter Tw
From Sharecropping to Shareholding—Going Public

Many small businesses have gone public, this is not new. But it becomes newsworthy when a black business is known to offer stock. One of the first black businesses in Harlem that I know of to have gone public was Inner City Broadcasting. The Honorable Percy Sutton offered me the opportunity to buy shares and I couldn't get the money to do so. I vowed that if the opportunity came about again, I would be ready. When Carver Bank went public, I bought stock. Sylvia's Restaurant followed, and for me, this was "the call."

I had been in pursuit of this road to the mainstream and had always believed that at its center was Wall Street. When I opened my business I was aware that it was not a "traditional" black business—a funeral home, restaurant, barber shop, etc.—and that because of that I would have a hard row to hoe, so to speak, but I was also aware that this type of business held great opportunity for expansion. As Sojourner Truth asked, "Ain't I a woman too?" I asked, "Can't a black woman own an office supply chain?"

I was depending on the Empowerment Zone funding to help bring me to a position where I could plan an investment project to empower our families. But *ces't la vie*, I am no stranger to advancing without the support of power structures. Many teachers: Moses, Sojourner, King, Gandhi, Malcolm and others have

Wall Street Financial Consultant Vernon Gibson and Dorothy Pitman Huges at conference where they participated in discussions on "how to create wealth among African Americans."

educated many of us in understanding where true power resides. I decided I would take advantage of whatever else was out there to get my agenda of real economic empowerment fulfilled. I went to Wall Street.

I began to look around at the growing small businesses around me. How did Starbuck's do it? I started to research the area. Someone suggested I meet a friend of theirs on Wall Street to help me get started, but when I went down to meet him, he wasn't at the office. Before leaving, I was directed to a back office, so I could get the ladies room key from the black woman there. She gave it to me and when I came back she inquired what my business was. I told her and she led me to a seat in the conference room, saying she'd like me to meet her son.

The woman was Doris Gibson, who works with me today, managing the stock operation for H.O.S., Inc. Her son is Vernon Gibson. He came into the conference room and Ms. Gibson told him to "help this lady." She explained to him that I had helped her when she lost her job at Harlem Hospital. She reminded me that she had come into Harlem Office Supply to get a resume done and had been very upset; that I had talked with her and comforted her, helping her to get through the problems she faced in losing her job. So this wonderful woman and her son guided me through the process of taking my business public and Ms. Gibson has been at my side, a great comfort and help to me in this endeavor.

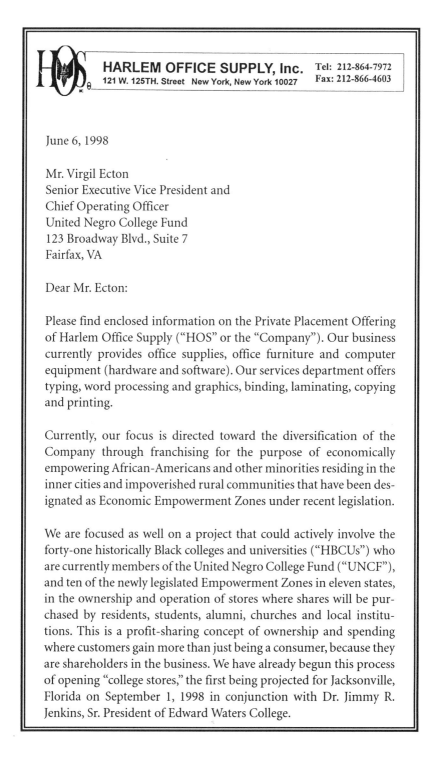

HARLEM OFFICE SUPPLY, Inc.
121 W. 125TH. Street   New York, New York 10027

Tel: 212-864-7972
Fax: 212-866-4603

June 6, 1998

Mr. Virgil Ecton
Senior Executive Vice President and
Chief Operating Officer
United Negro College Fund
123 Broadway Blvd., Suite 7
Fairfax, VA

Dear Mr. Ecton:

Please find enclosed information on the Private Placement Offering of Harlem Office Supply ("HOS" or the "Company"). Our business currently provides office supplies, office furniture and computer equipment (hardware and software). Our services department offers typing, word processing and graphics, binding, laminating, copying and printing.

Currently, our focus is directed toward the diversification of the Company through franchising for the purpose of economically empowering African-Americans and other minorities residing in the inner cities and impoverished rural communities that have been designated as Economic Empowerment Zones under recent legislation.

We are focused as well on a project that could actively involve the forty-one historically Black colleges and universities ("HBCUs") who are currently members of the United Negro College Fund ("UNCF"), and ten of the newly legislated Empowerment Zones in eleven states, in the ownership and operation of stores where shares will be purchased by residents, students, alumni, churches and local institutions. This is a profit-sharing concept of ownership and spending where customers gain more than just being a consumer, because they are shareholders in the business. We have already begun this process of opening "college stores," the first being projected for Jacksonville, Florida on September 1, 1998 in conjunction with Dr. Jimmy R. Jenkins, Sr. President of Edward Waters College.

To further expound on this concept, stores will be co-owned by the college or university and HOS, while offering shares at $1 per share to students, faculty, staff and families within the various communities throughout this network. HOS would offer the UNCF a promotional arrangement much like the one with McDonalds®, providing UNCF with another viable funding source of approximately 5%-7% of net revenues from each purchase by UNCF students.

By performing a "best effort offering" under the U.S. Securities and Exchange Commission's Regulation D-504 the provision would allow a store to raise capital by offering shares, with no set amount that has to be raised before it can start using the funds. Regulation D-504 also allows for the sale of securities to an unlimited amount of people.

There are tremendous opportunities associated with this undertaking, and we are seeking your assistance in getting UNCF member institutions to embrace this idea. I am requesting, with your help, the opportunity to share this concepts with the presidents of the UNCF member institutions. Their understanding and participation in this project is crucial to its success. They will have the unique opportunity to educate their students, faculty and community members about the intricacies of the stock market by providing low-cost hands-on involvement in business ownership through share holding and economic support. This is truly a learning experience in which the majority of today's African-American youth have never been involved. With over a trillion dollars a day being traded out of Wall Street, there should be no reason for today's African-American children to be unaware of the stock market and its processes.

Recently, Mr. Malcolm Corrin, Mr. Samuel P. Peabody (board member of TLC Beatrice Company and New York philanthropist) and I met with representatives from Solomon Smith Barney. We were asked by Smith Barney to upgrade our business plan to include the identification of areas we would like to focus on throughout the country. We would like to report in the business plan that we will have the participation of the HBCUs and the ten Empowerment Zones as our focus group. The representatives also stated that they were interested in assisting our effort by raising $3 to $5 million in working capital through their investment bankers, and that they are interested in taking our Company public.

The spending of the African-American community is massive, and Harlem Office Supply has been in the forefront by educating communities to recognize and use their own economic force as they move toward self-empowerment. The Reverend Jesse Jackson's efforts to open up the Wall Street community to minority entrepreneurs and investors have already strengthened our position.

We have made progress, but we are not yet satisfied. As you can see from the enclosed information, we are being looked at with some interest, both by national press and the Wall Street community, as we are determined that the playing field be leveled for minorities in the new millennium. Our children must have true equal opportunity to fully participate in the American dream to become professional people, politicians, educators and entrepreneurs, through improved education, environment, opportunity and economic empowerment.

The plan of opening a store on every campus is a win-win situation for all parties involved. For the community, it actively involves members in business ownership and entrepreneurial endeavors that impact and improve its economic standing. For HOS, it provides an avenue for growth as a successful and viable Black-owned and operated business along a road paved with community involvement, citizen support, and fiduciary responsibility. And for the UNCF, they become beneficiaries of a profitable venture that raises economic awareness of each individual community as well as providing educational opportunities for students who are interested in contributing to the economic empowerment of a people while pursuing the greatest American dream of entrepreneurism.

Your positive response to this innovative proposal could make a significant difference in the Empowerment Zone. We look forward to hearing from you.

Respectfully,

Dorothy Pitman Hughes
President and C.E.O.

Real Economic Empowerment

I had watched business after business close down in Harlem while distributors of EZ funds had carte blanche to use the fact that we weren't on par to "compete" with the already empowered companies coming in. We were told that it was a new day, that Harlem would be different now and if we weren't ready to compete, we should get out.

We are now having to contend with a different kind of power—not just racism, classism and sexism, but something new in our communities; this corporate fever that has hit all over the country. The idea of "compete, compete, compete" without regard for the context in which we are supposed to be competing. Any societal structure—government, business, education—exists as a system to serve humanity. This philosophy of competition for the sake of competition and open-ended growth is killing America. We, as African-Americans and other people of color in this country can ill afford to take it on. We are the last people in the position to buy this false, empty sense of power and think we can survive it.

Many people have wondered why I don't just take the many opportunities I've had to just throw the towel in and "look out for number one." The answer is that I know that there is no such thing as "number one". Any business endeavor I make is with a mind to how it serves my family and my community. There is no other way to think about it for me because the idea that it would be "worth it" or "cost effective" to put someone out of a job or cause any harm whatsoever to anyone in order to make more money would simply be an illusion. The cost of the downfall of a human being is always too high—let alone that of an entire community.

There is plenty of money to be made. What is money? We make money. We print it based on the level of desire and energy that we have to serve the welfare of humanity—or to exploit it. I would be deluding myself to think that my life was all about me. If it were, then God would have put me here by myself. But I am not alone, and therefore anything and everything I do affects someone else. So the choice is mine—do I want to affect people for the better, or for the worse? This is a serious question. And if one answers it "for the better" then one must do so with a firm resolve to make every action reflect that choice. As a businesswoman, the choice I made to grow my business only naturally involved the community.

Empowerment "From the Bottom Up"

Historically, black people have been invited to **participate** in the economic life of America, but not necessarily to **benefit** from that participation. Today, African-American consumers spend 500 Billion consumer dollars annually, but this major participation in the American economy benefits us and our children shamefully little, as "sharecropper" economics continues to plague our communities.

It is not that we do not **have** the power, it is that we do not **hold** the power. It slips through our fingers at a rate of 500 Billion dollars per year.

In1997 Harlem Office Supply, Inc. began a process by which members of our inner city and rural communities can begin to hold, and wield, some of the power that our dollars entitle us to. H.O.S., Inc. began offering shares to the people of our communities under the Security Exchange Commission's (SEC) 504 Regulation D plan. This is a Private Stock Offering under which a small company can offer "shares" or "stock" in its business and thereby raise funds to expand that business; with all of the stockholders, including the owner and principles in the business, profiting as the business grows and begins to show returns. It is a process by which the stockholders invest in the success of the business at the same time helping to insure the success of the business.

Offering stock in the business at only $1 per share, Harlem Office Supply, Inc. has made stockholders of people from as-yet-unborn babies to the most senior persons in the communities. There are over 1,700 children and 6,000 adult shareholders participating in this new movement for self-empowerment. And ownership is making a difference in their lives.

In Harlem, parents bring their children into our store and show them the physical reality of their participation in the American dream. When they leave the store they are less vulnerable to pushers and more motivated to develop and pursue their own dreams. Parents and children alike are becoming better educated about economics and how economics relate to their lives. And for the first time in a long time since emancipation and the right to vote was won, people are understanding that there is a **reason** to vote.

African-Americans across the country are inquiring with us about the possibility of establishing African-American mutual funds. Schools are inquiring from New York, New Jersey, Florida, South Carolina and Georgia. We have shareholders all the way in Saudi Arabia who read about us and quickly responded to support this movement for real empowerment.

The Education Minister of South Africa recently called me about modeling a program there after our stock offering; to educate and empower the children of South Africa and their families.

This movement for self-empowerment is possible in all of the designated Empowerment Zones. We intend to demonstrate the potency of an empowerment effort that empowers directly and for the long term; and with an eye to the immediate and tangible effect on both the psyche and the economic outlook of the people of the EZ communities and all urban and rural black communities.

The first group of children who became HOS shareholders after they became proud owners.

Chapter Thirteen
Putting "Stock" In Your Future

More and more of the traditional brokers are focusing on the African-American community with their advertisements. We may be glad we're being recognized, but caution: one should check the five year track record of any mutual funds being advertised to you or which you may be considering buying. These stocks may be building prisons for your children as opposed to the schools you need in your community.

When we put our money in the bank, that very day it becomes available to someone else or is very often being invested in something that is destructive to our community on a health, business, social or educational level. We may be using our own money to pay for our demise. Understand that money is always doing something; it's never just sitting around. Start to take responsibility for what your money is doing. Start making it work for *you*.

Do, however, invest wisely. When buying stock, check with the Securities Exchange Commission (SEC) or the State Attorney General's Office to see that the business is registered and legitimate. It is important that you trust the people you are dealing with when buying stock. Ask questions, make sure you understand the process; what your part in it is and what you can expect from the seller. Your investment can be the catalyst for creating an economic foundation for yourself, your family and your community.

Dorothy speaking at a 1998 shareholders meeting (a portion of Harlem Office Supply, Inc.'s 4,000 shareholders).

Trust = Funds

Let's expand, for a moment on "trust." As important as it is to deal with people you can trust, it is also important to be clear and make up your own mind about the general trustworthiness of black business.

Since the beginning of racial integration in this country the propaganda that black business is inferior to white business has infested our consciousness. Even our language implies inferiority; that we are "minorities." But we are not minorities in our own communities. We are very definitely the majority and our businesses should be thought of as the "major" factor in our success.

It is essential for many of our people that we take a deep look at just how much of this propaganda we have bought into. Recently, when a new Starbuck's store came into Harlem, a Black woman of some prominence was quoted in the Washington Post as saying, "Now we can finally get a good cup of coffee in Harlem." I take issue with the idea, first of all that there wasn't a good cup of coffee to be had in Harlem, but let's just say that somehow she's right, and no one in Harlem knows how to make a cup of coffee. A more important question is brought to my mind: What price would you pay for a good cup of coffee? If getting a good cup of coffee is worth losing a community then we have a real problem on our hands.

Offering memorandum

HARLEM OFFICE SUPPLY, INC.
A Maximum of 500,000 Shares
Offering Price—$1.00 per Share

Harlem Office Supply, Inc. (the "Company") hereby offer (the "Offering") a maximum of 500,000 Shares (each a "Share" and collectively the "Shares") of the Company's common stock (par value $0.00) per share ("Common Stock") at an offering price of $1.00 per Share (the "Offering Price") for an aggregate offering price of $500,000. The offering price of the Shares has been arbitrarily determined by the Company and bears no relationship to the assets or book value of the Company or any other recognized criteria of value.

Prior to this Offering there has been no public market for any securities of the Company and no assurances can be given that a market will develop for the Shares or, if developed, that it will be maintained after the Offering.

This Offering is being made pursuant to the exemption from the registration provisions of the Securities Act of 1933, as amended, afforded by Rule 504 of Regulation D promulgated thereunder and state small corporate offering registration provisions. Pursuant to said Rule 504, the securities sold hereby will not be subject to limitations the offer and sale and the resale of the Shares imposed by the Blue Sky laws of individual states.

THESE SECURITIES HAVE NOT BEEN APPROVED OR DISAPPROVED BY ANY FEDERAL OR STATE SECURITIES AGENCY NOR HAS ANY AGENCY REVIEWED OR PASSED UPON THE ACCURACY OR ADEQUACY OF THIS DISCLOSURE STATEMENT. ANY REPRESENTATION TO THE CONTRARY IS A CRIMINAL OFFENSE.

THE SECURITIES OFFERED HEREBY ARE HIGHLY SPECULATIVE, INVOLVE A HIGH DEGREE OF RISK, AND SHOULD BE PURCHASED ONLY BY PERSONS WHO CAN AFFORD TO LOSE THEIR ENTIRE INVESTMENT, ACCORDINGLY, INVESTORS MUST RELY UPON THEIR OWN EXAMINATION OF THIS OFFERING AND THE COMPANY IN MAKING AN INVESTMENT DECISION.

	Price to Public	Underwriting Discounts (1)	Proceeds to Company (2)
Per Share	$1	$0.10	$0.90
Total Maximum 500,000 Shares	$500,000	$50,000	$450,000

The date of this Offering Memorandum is May 15, 1997

Stock Consultant Ron Bookman addresses Harlem Office Supply, Inc. board members at a meeting held at the Black Enterprises board room regarding the HOS, Inc. public stock offer.

Chapter Fourteen
Dare To Be Free

"Our deepest fear is not that we are inadequate.
Our deepest fear is that we are powerful beyond measure.
It is our light, not our darkness, that most frightens us.
We ask ourselves, Who am I to be brilliant, gorgeous,
talented and fabulous?
*Actually, who are you **not** to be?*

You are a child of God.
Your playing small doesn't serve the world.
There is nothing enlightened about shrinking so that other
people won't feel insecure around you.
We are born to make manifest the glory of God that is within us.
It's not in just some of us; it's in everyone.
And as we let our own light shine, we unconsciously give
other people permission to do the same.
As we are liberated from our own fear, our presence
automatically liberates others."

Nelson Mandela
1994 Inaugural Speech

I do not know of any white company that has ever been criticized for expanding. Newspapers, local governments, residents, stockholders and consumers applaud when a small business opens a new store in a chain or expands an existing business site. In other words, when a small business gets bigger, offering more investment opportunities, more return on investment, more products, more job opportunities, etc., it is rightly considered good news for everyone. Not surprisingly, though, I have received some criticism, in this new EZ climate, for offering shares in my company to the community. "She is taking money from those poor people" is one I have heard.

First let me say that the SEC's 504 Reg. D was not invented for me. I've offered stock the same way any other company has, only **I've offered it to people whom some folks don't want owning stock.** Business, in this country, is based on dollars. There are very few businesses in this country, and no large businesses that do not have many, many stockholders. But how many of the millions of stockholders in this country are black? And how many are "poor"? The 504 D private stock offering was not put in place with me *or us* in mind, but when we start to use it for our own benefit somehow the time-honored process now becomes a process of "taking from the poor." The "poor" who spend billions of dollars every year making other people rich. What my shareholders are buying with that $1 a share is the beginning of control of self. What is Nike Corp. giving you on your "investment" of over $100 per pair of shoes? When those shoes are worn out, what do you have? Garbage. What does Nike have?—$100 and another hundred coming.

It is distressing to know that these criticisms are coming from my own people. I sometimes suffer, as many of us do, from the misguided expectation that black people should somehow be "better than that" just by virtue of the fact that they are black and have suffered injustice. But I think sometimes it is this very fact that catapults some into such fear that they would engage in hurting their own people.

Freedom carries an awesome responsibility. Not everyone has been fortunate enough to develop the fortitude and the courage to realize and embrace that responsibility. Because with it almost certainly comes sacrifice and pain. Sometimes the only pain is the pain of leaving an old perception of who you are or are *supposed to be*, behind. Sometimes the only sacrifice is the sense of security that the fear itself gives. If one clutches their fear, at least they know who they are, their "place." Freedom is a "great unknown" for many of us. And freedom requires one to take responsibility for their own life. How deadly are the fearful. How deadly it is to *be* fearful, because in fear one is *never* free.

Just tonight, before sitting down to finish this chapter, I was asked by a group to speak on their behalf because they are being forced out of their homes in Harlem. I sincerely hope that enough of us will wake up and begin to see what is happening in our communities and remove the veils of fear which, in the end, serve nothing and no one.

People all over this country are losing their jobs and homes because of the rapacious growth of large corporations. Harlem is one of the few communities that has remained virtually untouched by this corporate rampage. And despite the fact that we have it within our means to build and sustain an empowering economy for our community, we are *inviting* corporate America in to pillage, divide, and gentrify our historically black community which has sustained us through the years.

I am certain that the attitude and the excuse many of our people have for allowing our community to be taken away from us is that, 'that is how business works'. I am certain that this idea that 'business is business' is allowing many to rest quite content in the idea that there is nothing they can do about it—"it's the way of the world." Let me just remind us all of some of the people who chose not to put so little stock in the power of good and the power of humanity—and in the intelligence, ability and worthiness of poor and working people—that they would not themselves stand up and demand a different way:

Jesus Christ, Martin Luther King, Malcolm X, Sojourner Truth, Marcus Garvey, Rosa Parks, Mahatma Ghandi, Angela Davis, The Honorable Dorothy Height, The Honorable Percy E. Sutton, Lessie B. Ridley, Judge Bruce Wright, Justice Thurgood Marshall, Shirley Chisholm,

Patrice Lumumba, Nelson and Winnie Mandela, John Beatty, Anne Wells, Calvin Copeland, Prof. Preston Wilcox, Atty. Edward Fordham, Florence R. Kennedy, Florence Rice, Queen Mother Moore, Reverend Al Sharpton, Ms. Alma John, Sam Peabody, Archbishop Desmond Tutu, Fannie Lou Hamer, Adam Clayton Powell, Jr., Booker T. Washington, Prof. John Henry Clark, W.E.B. DuBois, James Weldon Johnson, Dr. Ben, Esther Williams, Medgar Evers, Silas McGee, Reverend Jessie Jackson, Gloria Steinem, Reva L. Sharoth, and many, many others.

There are many new companies using business to further agendas which serve their consumers, stockholders and the community at large. There are companies which invest only in businesses that manufacture goods in America; that give large percentages of their profits to non-profit social organizations; that do business only with ecologically and socially responsible businesses. Many people are waking up to the fact that where one puts one's money is where one gives one's power. It is not impossible to be conscious and successful at the same time. In fact it is necessary.

HOW I DID IT: GOING PUBLIC IN HARLEM

Like many small-business owners, Dorothy Pitman Hughes mortgaged her house to finance her business when she opened the Harlem Copy Center in 1985. The copy center has since grown into Harlem Office Supply, Inc., a full-service retail operation that sells computers, fax machines and office furniture. It did more than $300,000 in sales last year. What has also expanded is how Hughes now raises capital. Instead of tapping real estate, she has looked to Wall Street and is taking her company public, using a little-known regulation of the U.S. Securities and Exchange Commission (SEC) that makes it easier for small businesses to raise capital by offering stock shares. Hughes plans to raise $2 million by the year 2000 by offering stock for $1 a share. Here's how she's doing it:

THE OFFERING: "We're doing what's called a 'best effort offering' under the SEC's Regulation D504. With the D504 you can raise up to $1 million in a 12-month period, and there is no set amount that has to be raised before you can start using the funds. You can also sell securities to an unlimited number of people."

THE COST: "Setting up this stock offering cost about $50,000, using a lawyer who specializes in private placement offerings—which means putting together an offering document that gives part of the balance sheet of the company. You then have to register or file to trade the shares with your state's securities regulator, and this costs about $800. Once you file, you get a symbol that indicates the name under which your shares or stock are trading."

THE INVESTORS: "Anybody can buy stock in my company, which sells for $1 per share. The minimum for adults is 50 shares, and for children 25 shares. I want people in the Harlem community owning a piece of the business, so we'll have a place where our people—especially our children—can learn to understand stocks and bonds. A trillion dollars a day is traded out of Wall Street, and there's no way a child in this city shouldn't know about the stock market."

THE ECONOMICS: 'We currently have more than 4,000 shareholders with more than 350,000 shares, but until we go public, we're not paying dividends. For the offering to be successful, shareholders have to support the business with their buying dollar. By the year 2000, we hope to have three more stores in the New York metropolitan area."

For more information on taking a company public, contact the Securities and Exchange Commission, (202) 942-4046, and ask for the free pamphlet "Q&A: Small Business and the SEC-Help Your Company Go Public."

ESSENCE MAY 1998

EXTRA!! EXTRA!! WHILE WALL STREET PLUMMETS...

HARLEM OFFICE SUPPLY INC STOCK REMAINS STABLE AT ONLY $1 @ SHARE

New York—October 1997 - Amidst all the turmoil of the stock market turnaround, a Harlem entrepreneur calmly counts her blessings. Ms. Dorothy Pitman Hughes who is the first and only Black female member of SANY (Stationer's Association of New York) is no stranger to economic change. She opened her business fifteen years ago and is moving her Harlem Office Supply, Inc. towards a new chapter. With HOS Inc.'s goals of statewide and national expansion, the shareholders hope to be able to turn their investments of $1 a share into a vehicle for their personal economic empowerment.

As Harlem Office Supply, Inc. located at 121 West 125th Street opened its doors this morning, a customer walked in for the sole purpose of making an "over-the-counter" purchase of shares. She stated to Ms. Hughes "Since the market is down, I want to buy low here. This might be the only investment that pays off today." Once she had made her purchase of fifty shares, Ms. Davis remarked "These kind of stores need to survive. They give personal service and now when I buy I'll know I'm investing in MY store.

Ms. Davis is one of over 2000 HOS, Inc. shareholders who are investing in their own uptown business and contributing to the store's growth and therefore, their own equity by purchasing their stationary items, office supplies, office furniture, computers and copies there.

For Dorothy Pitman Hughes, the market has remained stable and continues to increase. Buying low is the smart way to go.

The New York Amsterdam News
Vol. 88 No. 39 September 25-October 1, 1997

The new Black view
125th Street: A corridor of history

Dear Editor:

Harlem's 125th Street, its main strip, has been the site of several globally impacting news events. Joe Louis' knockout of Max Schneling on Wednesday, June, 22, 1938, was such an event. Another occurred on June, 20, 1990, when Nelson and Winnie Mandela came to, mark the return of the Prodigal Son to freedom.

The event which occurred at the Victoria 5 Theater, 235 W. 125th St. under the sponsorship of Harlem Office Supply, Inc. 121 W. 125th St., was not as charismatic as a media event, but it is equally as historical but, more importantly, self-empowering. It will slowly begin to change the negative ideological view of capitalism by replacing it with a participating experience which involves both economic and educational aspect—using our own money.

The ground-level movie level movie theater was jammed, not with radical ideologues, designer-model individuals—or people looking for still another handout or freebee, Most of them had not been seen at any of Harlem's extraordinary number of gatherings. There's always a meeting taking place in Harlem—in a school, a church basement, a beauty parlor, a saloon, a barbershop, an eating establishment, etc. But these were not meeting-goers; they were meeting doers. They came to participate, to contribute, to listen and learn and to: Put their money where their mouth is," for they came to take care of serious business—to purchase shares in Harlem Office Supply, Inc. at $1 per share!

This reporter had his own expectations overshadowed by the response. I doubted that the amount finally raised was even a slight possibility. When all was said and done, Harlem Office Supply, Inc. had raised $85,000. Yes. $85,000 on Monday, Sept. 15, in Harlem!

Preston Wilcox

Amsterdam News

Harlem Office Supplies to initiate stock offering

NEW YORK - Harlem Office Supplies has accepted the challenge to empower the people or their community by offering them the opportunity to own shares of the business. While it is noted that there is not one chain of stores owned by African-Americans in the Harlem area, Harlem Office Supplies vows to change these statistics. This opportunity of ownership comes 30 years after the Civil Rights Movement and 14 years after Harlem Office Supplies opened its doors for business.

Located at 121 West 125th St., Harlem Office Supplies has become one of Harlem's and New York City's foremost suppliers of office products, school supplies and services—including typing and word processing. Because of the loyalty of its many customers, vast community support and a vision to empower the people of many inner cities across the country, Harlem Office Supplies has been put in the position of being able to sell 500,000 shares of stock for $1 a share, over-the-counter to all those who wish to experience the pride of ownership of a business and share in their profits.

Children are a particular focal point in this drive so that they can fulfill their dreams of paying their own way through college, buying a co-op or condominium, or traveling around the world. Because the education system does not teach inner-city children about stocks and bonds, Harlem Office Supplies invites all community leaders, schools and churches to become involved in the teaching and purchasing of stocks so that our children will have a new Harlem for a new century.

Entrepreneur
Volume 27, No. 2

Neighborhood Watch

When taking care of the community means taking care of business
New York City entrepreneur Dorothy Pitman Hughes was on a mission. After years of supporting local economic empowerment efforts, in late 1997, the owner of Harlem Office Supply Inc. decided to take her involvement to a whole new level.

Her goal? To educate black youths on the power of investing. But her teaching method was virtually unheard of in her Harlem community. Hughes began selling shares of her company stock for $1 per share.

"We were shocked at the response," she says. Hughes sold 85,000 shares in the offering's first week, fueled by an advertising drive in local media and churches.

The SEC 504(d) over-the-counter offering has enabled Hughes to expand her business, but she says her real reward is in giving Harlem's future entrepreneurs a taste of business ownership through their stock purchases. Parents drop their kids off for the Saturday morning investment classes Hughes holds for students aged 6 to 15. If they can save up $125 for sneakers, she counsels, they can also save for their futures by investing. "[The] children are really beginning to understand it," says Hughes.

And the trend is catching on at all age levels: With nearly $400,000 in total shares sold and more than 5,000 shareholders, community members are even registering their babies for shares and giving shares instead of traditional gifts at baby showers.

Hughes' goal is to take Harlem Office Supply public on January 1, 2000. "It's become more like a crusade," she says of her unique win-win approach. And she's spreading the word: "It's a prototype [for entrepreneurs] that can [benefit youths] nationwide."

—Elaine W. Teague

THE NEW YORK AMSTERDAM NEWS

March 19-March 25, 1998

Harlem store offers shares to its faithful

By Yvonne Delaney
Special to the AmNews

The Harlem Office Supply Store on 125th Street has more to offer than just the standard office fare. They are now offering shares in the business as they prepare to march into the millennium with the big boys of Wall Street. To date, there are close to 4,000 HOS Inc. shareholders and over 100 of them met on March 15 for their first shareholders meeting.

The idea of owning shares in a business is revolutionary to some, yet a part of life to the corporation counterparts, who exist on the other side of Central Park. Part of the shareholders meeting's focus was to break down this barrier and dispel the myth that dealing in high finance is above the heads of minorities and the "lower" class. According to Dorothy Pitman Hughes, owner of HOS, "We have been left out of the economic mainstream. In order to have real economic power, we must empower ourselves."

The meeting was held at the Riverbank Cultural Building Theatre Complex on 145th Street. Dr. Bob Law, WWRL Radio program director, was the emcee and special guest speaker. Other featured speakers were the Rev. Dennis Dillon, publisher of New York Christian Times and Dr. Jimmy R. Jenkins, president of Edward Waters College in Florida.

Hughes' commitment toward economic development is an inspiration. "It isn't that we don't have money, but we spend it back with the very people that we work for, from food to clothing and rent and we have nothing to show for it. We must end this vicious cycle. Secondly, we are calling on the Board of Education to institute projects to teach our children the mechanics behind trading and owning stocks and bonds."

Hughes believes it's important to work with the youths, in getting them involved, for they are the real movers and shakers of the future. HOS's aim is to make shareholders of 5,000 youths by the year 2000.

She is well on her way toward reaching this goal as seen by members from the Brooklyn Economical Youth Credit Union, who attended the meeting and purchased a significant number of shares. Receiving 1,000 shares each were Dion and Dinelle Maxwell, winners of the "Student Essay Awards Competition." Contestants were asked to write an essay depicting what they knew about stocks and bonds. Indications were clear, if given the opportunity and exposure, these students will be future Wall Street inhabitants.

"Without economic equality, there is no social or political equality. Malcom X, Madame C.J. Walker, the Rev. Martin Luther King Jr. all brought us through the Red Sea. We are now on the other side of the civil rights movement. It's time for us to create the kind of environment and educational system we want." Anyone interested in finding out more information on purchasing shares can stop by the store where financial experts will explain the details.

5th Issue 1997 Reprinted from "STREET NEWS" written by Indio

"ECONOMIC EMPOWERMENT TEAM OF HARLEM STANDS UP"

Harlem Office Supply, Inc. has accepted the challenge to empower the people of their community by offering them the opportunity to own shares of the business. while it is noted that there is not one chain of stores owned by African-Americans in the Harlem area, Harlem Office Supply, Inc. vows to change these statistics. This opportunity of ownership comes 30 years after the Civil Rights Movement and 14 years after Harlem Office Supply, Inc. opened its doors for business. Located at 6 East 125th Street, Harlem Office Supply, Inc. has become one of Harlem's and New York City's foremost suppliers of office products, school supplies and services including typing and word processing. Because of the loyalty of its many customers, vast community support and a vision to empower the people of many inner cities across the country, Harlem Office supply, Inc. has been put in the position of being able to sell 500,000 shares of stock for $1 a share, over the counter to all those who wish to experience the pride of ownership of a business and share in its profits.

Children are a particular focal point in this drive so that they can fulfill their dreams of paying their own way through college, buying a co-op or condominium, or traveling around the world. Because the education system does not teach inner city children about stocks and bonds, Harlem Office Supply, Inc. invites all Community Leaders, Schools and Churches to become involved in the teaching and purchasing of stocks so that our children will have a new Harlem for a new century.

Ms. Dorothy Pitman Hughes has been the recipient of many civic and community awards and a key fundraiser for several political campaigns. The media has also highly recognized Dorothy for her many contributions. Her most recent appearances were on "The Roland Watts Show," "The Channel 11 News," New York 1 News" and "The Gil Nobel's 'Like It Is' Show," in which she enlightened the community about the Harlem Empowerment Zone and "The Leezah Show," where she was invited to appear because of her similarities to the lead character in the movie "The Associate." Like the character, Ms. Hughes has also managed to break down the barriers in Harlem and around wall street. With this awareness, many community residents have rushed to purchase those shares some have spent $1; some have spent $5,000. You can check them out by making a visit or call (212) 427-3540 or fax (212) 427-3816.

4000 SHAREHOLDERS TO RECEIVE UPDATE ABOUT THEIR HARLEM OFFICE SUPPLY, INC. STOCK

Sunday, March 15, 1998 at 2: 00 P.M. Ms. Dorothy Pitman Hughes will present Harlem Office Supply, Inc.'s 1st Annual ShareHolders Meeting. Four thousand NOS, Inc. shareholders have been invited to attend this historic event which will take place at Riverbank Cultural Building Theatre Complex, 679 Riverside Drive (145th Street), New York.

The M.C. and Special Guest Speaker for the event will be WWRL-Radio's Program Director Bob Law (former "Night Talk" Host). Other Featured Speakers will be Reverend Dennis Dillon, Publisher of New York Christian Times and Dr. Jimmy R. Jenkins, President of Edward Waters College, Jacksonville, Florida. A Special Presentation of 1000 Shares Harlem Office Supply, Inc.'s Stock will be made to the winners of the "Student Essay Awards Competition". Live Gospel Music will add a spiritual lift to the day's events.

It is expected that, of the 4000 shareholders, several hundred will show up to hear when and how these stocks will be taken to the market for trade. The "Economic Empowering Movement" is creating quite a stir throughout the country and calls are already coming in from youth sponsored groups in South Carolina, and Black colleges in the South. The first to own a partnership with Harlem Office Supply, Inc. will be the Edward Waters College of Jacksonville, Florida. Like the group of business owners that Reverend Dillon brought to open over a million dollars in accounts to Carver Bank, the Brooklyn Economical Youth Credit Union has shown interest in attending this meeting to purchase a significant amount of shares. It is obvious that Harlem Office Supply's movement to empower 5000 youth before the year 2000 is well on its way to becoming the success planned.

Ms. Hughes, who has been an advocate for the "Economic Empowerment" movement, has received national media recognition for her accomplishments. Fifteen years ago, she planned, opened, and organized Harlem Office Supply, Inc. and has become one of Harlem's anchors in business. She has received numerous requests to assist other entrepreneurs who wish to take their small businesses public.

Business Woman/Community Activist Honored On Oprah Show

By Arn Ashwood

Dorothy Hughes, the founder and president of Harlem Office Supplies, has been listening to a different drummer all her life. "Economic freedom forms the framework for everything that I do. Once you achieve economic freedom, you will achieve social and political freedom. People sometimes find my attitude hard to understand," she smiles, "but it's simply that I refuse to accept my limitations."

Eighteen years ago a limitation motivated her to start a business in Harlem. "I had bought a house in Harlem and one day needed to make a copy of a document. There was no place in the whole neighborhood to get a copy made." She immediately recognized an opportunity. "I went home and told my kids that we were starting a business."

She started a copy service, then branched out into a full service retail operation that sells stationary and office supplies. In the years since she started, her industry has experienced explosive growth, with expansive globalization through technological advances. "This is a business with incredible growth potential. And I realized that Harlem Office Supplies is perfectly positioned to expand as this industry expands."

Along with this realization came another, She would need a lot of capital to take advantage of this opportunity. That's when Dorothy Hughes had a breakthrough revelation:

Dorothy Pitman Hughes (seated left of Oprah) recently appeared on The Oprah Winfrey "Great Moms" salute show To get the money she would follow the money. "If you honestly look at where the money flows in this community you'll see a peculiar path. When we spend money here, it doesn't stay here. It goes out, and if you follow that path you'd see that money eventually ends up on Wall Street. That's where we needed to go to get it back."

Dr. Jimmy Jenkins, President of Edward Waters College in Jacksonville, Florida with Dorothy Pitman Hughes. Edward Waters College will be the first Black college campus to have a Harlem Office Supply store under the College Expansion Program.

Chapter Fifteen
Onward...

*"Nothing else in the world...not all the armies...
is so powerful as an idea whose time has come."*

Victor Hugo

Harlem Office Supply, Inc. is planning a major, nationwide expansion. I have met with several groups, including the Teamsters' National Black Caucus, who have agreed to join us in making shareholders of the people of our communities. These like-minded and formidable groups have expressed their recognition of some of the same concerns as I have mentioned in this book and they are prepared to join me in taking major action to establish, through the H.O.S., Inc. plan, a process of real economic empowerment for our communities.

I Believe We Are Our Children's Future

One of the reasons I set the initial stock offering for my business at only $1 per share is that it was important to me to have children purchase stock in my company. Our goal at Harlem Office Supply, Inc. is go to Wall Street with a noticeable number of black children holding stock.

Our aim is to end the cycle of dollars being hemorrhaged out of our communities and away from our children. "Ownership" is the element that distinguishes Black communities from what would otherwise just be "Black ghettos." I am determined that the

The first group of Harlem Office Supply, Inc.'s children to purchase HOS, Inc. stock at $1 per share.

next generations of our children will come into adulthood with a stake in their community—and that their community will therefore have a stake in them—creating a new cycle of economic and social nurturance and empowerment.

Many of us have worked very hard to give our children a better life than we had. We have cultivated what on the surface looks like a middle class life; even though many of us are living dollar to dollar, without a dollar to spare. But when we invest in the illusion of a middle class life—the nice home, good education, good clothes, the latest video games and expensive sneakers—and we don't invest in a plan for our children's economic future, we are really giving them a false sense of security.

Our children grow up with middle class values but unlike their counterparts in other cultures, they don't have the economic base to support those values. And what this so often does is leaves everyone frustrated. We wonder why our children act like money grows on trees. Why they don't understand how hard we have to work for it. But we're the ones giving it to them without engaging them in the process or educating them in how that money works or is cultivated. So often the fact is that **we** don't understand. And we're part of that same syndrome that has kept us going one step forward and two steps back.

What our middle and working class counterparts in other cultures do that we, as a rule, have not done is put "stock" in their children's future. Their kids pay tuitions, start businesses and careers and buy their first homes with stocks that their parents, grandparents, aunts and uncles bought them years ago.

So much ambition is lost when you have to struggle to survive. The secret other cultures have understood for generations is Investment. No one gets anywhere without a helping hand from someone else, especially our children. There is not one success story to be found in which that success was reached alone. And the "rags to riches" story—although pushed to and celebrated in our communities—is very rare.

We are our children's future. The opportunities they have in their young adulthood will directly reflect the decisions we make now. If our community is to survive, the people of our communities must survive and remain connected to the community. Our community's success depends on the energy, the knowledge, the decision-making and the actions that we take as **individuals**. It is up to each one of us be conscious and alert; to *Wake Up and Smell the Dollars*!

What You Can Do

Buy into or help organize a business that is needed in our community. Invest in it, invite others to invest in it, watch it grow and enjoy the returns. There are no restrictions on 504 D stock so

*Dorothy Pitman Hughes proudly introduces her grandson,
Sean Ridley, to attendees at the 1998 Harlem Office Supply,
Inc. shareholders meeting.*

even your baby can own shares through the program. When
buying stock, check with the Security Exchange Commission
(SEC) or the State Attorney to see that the business is registered
and legitimate.

The next baby shower you have, register for stocks instead of at a
clothing or toy store. The next shower you are invited to, show up
with stock, so the baby comes into the next century owning
something. The next wedding, send stock; give them a future. For

Kwanza, Christmas, Hanukkah; give the gift of freedom by stuffing stocks in their stockings. Next time you want to smile on a friend with a gift, don't buy a trinket—put stock in their future!

I am confident that H.O.S, Inc.'s Ownership Initiative will be a rallying point, with shareholders coming together to better their communities: to create voting blocks whereby the citizenry will build better schools and care for the infrastructures of our communities; to block out crime and create villages in which to raise our children. My experience with our pioneers, the first nearly 8,000 shareholders of H.O.S., Inc., supports my belief that the economic empowerment of our communities **will** occur, and that our shareholders will be the bridge that takes us from sharecropping to shareholding in the new millennium.

I urge business owners to look into the 504 D Plan. Get involved. Prepare to build a foundation for real empowerment. **Wake up and smell the dollars!**

The Future Is Now

I was most pleased with something my eleven year old grandson, Sean Ridley, did this past summer. He came home one day from day camp, where I knew he was working on his basketball skills for the upcoming school year. He announced that he had been voted President of the Economics Group at camp. We all congratulated him and then asked how he had won the election. What had he said in his speech? He said, "Grandma, I told them about buying stock. I asked if they owned stock in Nike, or Play Station, or any of the games we love to play. They all said 'no', and I said, 'we should! If we are buying these products. But better yet we need to set up our own companies and economically empower ourselves!" He served his presidential term at camp and continued honing his basketball skills. We're all very confident he'll do well in basketball…and in the stock market, and in anything else he chooses.

Dorothy Pitman Hughes at home today.

Chapter Sixteen
Conclusion

The salient economic fact in all our lives in this century will be the growing economic gap between the haves and the have nots. That's where we're headed, it's clear. It is also clear that if people don't see economic opportunity, they drop out of society. As the racial make-up of this country changes, and the non-white population grows, the nation's well-being and **our** well-being will depend on whether this growth widens the economic gap between the races, or helps to close it.

As consumers, as taxpayers, and as workers we must look at and take responsibility for where our money is going and what it is doing. Where is our money being invested?—our workers' benefits, taxes and savings? In many cases that money is going toward building industries which do not serve us as a community. The prison industry is one such industry, and the most stark example of how we are helping to underwrite our own demise.

The prison population statistics of today show that prisons are overflowing with hugely and offensively disproportionate numbers of black men, women and children. It is clear that it is **our** children who will increasingly inhabit these prisons as the economic climate in this country becomes more competitive and our communities become less self-sufficient through the closings of community-based businesses.

I submit the most fundamental level of need in our communities is ownership and entrepreneurism. The EZ has failed to focus on an empowerment that would be guided upward, from the bottom to the top, as was its stated intention, but rather has attached itself to a "trickle down" process which history has shown serves none but the already empowered. Both the Great Depression and the economic destruction of the Reagan era were a result of this philosophy.

Recently as many as 22 black-owned businesses have closed down within a 30 block radius of Harlem's center. The loss to the community is not merely a few jobs or the products and services the businesses offered—in some cases they will be replaced by large corporations—but what leaves with those businesses is both the economic and social basis for a truly "empowered" community of people.

Just as ownership and entrepreneurism was the basic means of our survival after slavery and during the years of "Jim Crow," ownership and entrepreneurism will be our means of recovery from the loss of our businesses after integration. Ownership and entrepreneurism will allow us to establish social, economic and political power in our lives and the lives of our children in the next century.

Mainstream America as well as much of the African-American community is losing patience with social programs and government "caretaking." As this sentiment grows so does the number of people in poverty. But America remains one of the richest countries in the world. America remains a land of opportunity. We must work to ensure that those opportunities for economic well-being remain open to us—as they are now if we choose to open our eyes and do what we must to take those opportunities. *Wake up and smell the dollars.*
                                                    —Dorothy Pitman Hughes

Appendix A
Should My Company Go Public?

When your company needs additional capital, "going public" may be the right choice, but you should weigh your options carefully. If your company is in the very early stages of development, it may be better to seek loans from financial institutions for the Small Business Administration. Other alternatives include raising money by selling securities in transactions that are exempt from the registration process.

There are benefits and new obligations that come from raising capital through a public offering with the SEC, While the benefits are attractive, be sure you are ready to assume these new obligations.

Benefits

▼ Your access to capital will increase, since you can contact more potential investors.

▼ Your company may become more widely known.

▼ You may obtain financing more easily in the future if investor interest in your company grows enough to sustain a secondary trading market in your securities.

▼ Controlling shareholders, such as the company's officers or directors, may have a ready market for their shares, which means they can more easily sell their interests at retirement, for diversification, or for some other reason.

▼ Your company may be able to attract and retain more highly qualified personnel if it can offer stock options, bonuses, or other incentives with a known market value.

▼ The image of your company may be improved.

New Obligations

▼ You must continue to keep shareholders informed about the company's business operations, financial condition, and management, incurring additional costs and new legal obligations.

▼ You may be liable if you do not fulfill these new legal obligations.

▼ You may lose some flexibility in managing your company's affairs, particularly when shareholders must approve your actions.

▼ Your public offering will take time and money to accomplish.

Where can I Go for More Information?

The staff of the SEC's Office of Small Business and the SEC's Small Business Ombudsman will be glad to assist you with any questions you may have regarding federal securities laws. For information about state securities laws, contact NASAA or your state's securities administrator, whose office is usually located in your capital city.

The entire text of the SEC's rules and regulations is available through the U.S. Government Printing Office or from several private publishers of legal information. In addition, numerous books on this subject have been published, and some are available in public libraries. As of this writing, the following volumes of

Title 17 of the Code of federal Regulations (the SEC's rules and regulations) were available from the Government Printing Office.

▼ Volume II—Parts 200 to 239, SEC Organization; Conduct and Ethics; Information and Requests; Rules of Practice; Regulation S-X and Securities Act of 1933.

▼ Volume III—Parts 240 to End. Securities Exchange Act of 1934; Public Utility Holding Company, Trust Indenture, Investment Company, Investment Advisers, and Securities, Investor protection Corporation Acts.

For additional information about how to obtain official publications of Commission rules and regulations, contact:

Superintendent of Documents
Government Printing Office
Washington, DC 20402-9325

For copies of SEC forms and recent SEC releases:

Publications Section
U.S. Securities and Exchange Commission
495 Fifth St. N.W., Stop C-11
Washington, DC 20549
Telephone (202) 942-4046

Other useful addresses, telephone Numbers, Web sites and e-mail:

SEC's World Wide Web site:
http://www.sec.gov

SEC Office of Small Business
SEC Small Business Ombudsman
U.S. Securities and Exchange Commission
450 Fifth Street, N.W., Stop 7-8
Washington, DC 20549
Telephone: (202) 942-2950
E-mail addresses:
  e-prospectus@sec.gov
  help@sec.gov

North American Securities Administrators Association
One Massachusetts Avenue, N.W., Suite 310
Washington, DC 20001
(202) 737-0900
NASAA's World Wide Web site:
http://www.nasaa.org

SBA's World Wide Web site:
http://www.sba.gov//ADVO

ACE-Net World Wide Web Site:
https://ace-net.sr.unh.edu

What it Takes to Do a 504 D Private Stock Offering

(The Master Plan in Easy Steps)

For some of you, your business may be ready to move right into the stock market. If so, and if you know so, here is where you may start. In your state you can:

1. Obtain a document called "Blue Sky".

2. Visit your State Department of Law. Pick up a Broker—Deals and Securities Regulation Information sheet.

3. Get instructions for filing a Designation Service of Process Pursuant to sections 352-a or 352-b of the General business Law of the State of New York.

4. Pick up Amendments to Security Transactions and Personal Regulations Chapter II Securities Transactions and Personnel Part 10: Brokers, Dealers, and Salespersons.

5. Get a State Department of Law Issuer Statement (Section 359e, General Business law) New York Form M-11.

6. Hire an attorney to facilitate a regulation D-504 Private Placement Equity offering Memorandum.
    a. Description of the company
    b. Risk Factors modified to specifics of the company
    c. Description of securities offered.
    d. Plan of distribution
    e. Capitalization calculations
    f. Use of proceeds summary
    g. Description of management/principals/shareholders
    h. Financials (when submitted)/summary
    i. Subscriptions agreement

Now, prepare documentation needed to format the offering. The following pages include some of the information from HOS, Inc.'s *Stock Offering Memorandum.* I hope that this will give you a clear direction towards completing the process of your stock offering.

Investment Made Small
To Empower Us All

Stock Offering

Harlem Office Supply, Inc.
121 West 125th Street
New York, NY 10027
(212) 866-4603

The Company

Harlem Office Supply, Inc.:

- was incorporated on May 15, 1992;

- is located in the heart of Harlem's bustling commercial center;

- has enjoyed steady growth by offering quality products at reasonable prices;

- offers coping, printing, word processing and typesetting services to small and medium-sized businesses, government offices, schools, students and the general public;

- plans to increase its market penetration with extensive network activities through the distribution of flyers and catalogs; and

- has launched a public relations campaign to secure local and national publicity via newspapers, magazines, radio, television, and the internet.

The President

Dorothy Pitman Hughes

- heads the Company as President and CEO;

- is dedicated to creating processing economic opportunities for her community;

- has a long and varied history as a developer, organizer and' director of successful enterprises;

- has over 30 years of business experience;

- is the first African American woman to become a member of the Stationers' Association of New York, and

- was a member of the Harlem Empowerment Zone Economic Development Committee.

- is a member of several organizations including:
  — Harlem Business Alliance
  — Black Women Enterprises
  — The National Black Women's Political Congress
  — The National Council of Negro Women
  — The National Organization for Women
  — Women Initiating Self Empowerment
  — Governor Task Force for Rape
  — The United States Peace Corps

- has owned and operated three day care centers;

- has sponsored a successful youth entrepreneur apprentice project; and

- Spent three years as a public speaker on the university circuit.

Stock Offering

Harlem Office Supply, Inc.:

- has responded to the challenge of economically empowering people in various communities throughout the country by becoming certified to offer 2,000,000 shares at $1 per share, thereby creating a public market for securities of the Company where one did not previously exist under SEC Rule 504 Regulation D;

- provides annual financial statements prepared by independent certified accountants as well as audited quarterly financial reports;

- plans to register with NASDAQ on June 1, 2000;

- plans to participate in share swaps with other major corporations in the Harlem community to bolster share purchases;

- offers a plan to directly target the nation's Empowerment Zones so that its residents may benefit from the economic education and stabilization of members in the inner city communities.

The HOS Plan

Harlem Office Supply, Inc.:

- plans to encourage and educate members of various communities to become economically empowered entrepreneurs and consumers;

- is focused on educating community youths about the stock market through hands-on experience through stock ownership;

- plans to enroll 5,000 African American children as shareholders by the year 2000;

- is focused on providing an example of how consumers can become owners by encouraging share ownership via franchise stores on college campuses and within inner city communities;

HBCU Initiative

Harlem Office Supply, Inc.:

- has met with the C.O.O. of the United Negro College Fund ("UNCF") to discuss plans to bring to each of the 41 Historical Black Colleges and Universities ("HBCU") a partnership store on each of their respective campuses;

- has provided the UNCF with a plan that would encourage students, faculty, alumni and members of the communities surrounding each HBCU to become owners of each store through stock ownership;

- has initiated this program through the opening of its flagship college store at Edward Waters College in Jacksonville, Florida this Fall;

- has received the full cooperation of President Jimmy Jenkins and Bishop Cummings of Edward Waters College in the initiation of this project;

- has received its first challenge grant from Mr. Pete Carpenter, President of CSX Transportation to match students' purchases of up to $10,000 in shares.

Urban Empowerment Zones & Enterprise Communities

Empowerment Zone (EZ)

- ▼ Georgia: Atlanta
- ▼ Illinois: Chicago
- ▼ Maryland: Baltimore
- ▼ New York: New York, Bronx County
- ▼ Pennsylvania: Philadelphia/Camden, NJ

Supplemental Empowerment Zone (SEZ)

- ▼ California: Los Angeles City & County
- ▼ Ohio: Cleveland

Enhanced Enterprise Community (EEC)

- ▼ California: Oakland
- ▼ Massachusetts: Boston
- ▼ Missouri: Kansas city (MO) and (KS)
- ▼ Texas: Houston

Enterprise Community

- ▼ Alabama: Birmingham
- ▼ Arizona: Phoenix
- ▼ Arkansas: Pulaski County/Little Rock
- ▼ California: Los Angeles/Huntington Park
- ▼ California: San Diego
- ▼ California: San Francisco/Bayview/Hunters Point
- ▼ Colorado: Denver
- ▼ Connecticut: Bridgeport
- ▼ Connecticut: New Haven
- ▼ Delaware: Wilmington
- ▼ District of Columbia: Washington
- ▼ Florida: Dade County, Miami
- ▼ Georgia: Albany
- ▼ Illinois: East St. Louis, Springfield

- ▼ Indiana: Indianapolis
- ▼ Iowa: Des Moines
- ▼ Kentucky: Louisville
- ▼ Louisiana: New Orleans, Ouachita Parish
- ▼ Massachusetts: Lowell, Springfield
- ▼ Michigan: Flint, Muskegon
- ▼ Minnesota: Minneapolis, St. Paul
- ▼ Mississippi: Jackson
- ▼ Missouri: St. Louis
- ▼ Nebraska: Omaha
- ▼ Nevada: Clark County/Las Vegas
- ▼ New Hampshire: Manchester
- ▼ New Jersey: Newark
- ▼ New Mexico: Albuquerque
- ▼ New York: Albany, Buffalo, Newburgh/Kingston, Rochester, Schenectady, Troy
- ▼ North Carolina: Charlotte
- ▼ Ohio: Akron, Columbus
- ▼ Oklahoma: Oklahoma City
- ▼ Oregon: Portland
- ▼ Pennsylvania: Harrisburg, Pittsburgh
- ▼ Rhode Island: Providence
- ▼ South Carolina: Charleston
- ▼ Tennessee: Memphis, Nashville
- ▼ Texas: Dallas, El Paso, San Antonio, Waco
- ▼ Utah: Ogden
- ▼ Vermont: Burlington
- ▼ Virginia: Norfolk
- ▼ Washington: Seattle, Tacoma
- ▼ West Virginia: Huntington
- ▼ Wisconsin: Milwaukee

Rural Empowerment Zones

▼ Kentucky: Kentucky Highlands
▼ Mississippi: Mid Delta
▼ Texas, Rio Grande Valley

Rural Enterprise Communities

Alabama: Chambers County, Greene and Sumter Counties
▼ Arizona Border Region
▼ Arkansas: East Central, Mississippi County
▼ California: Imperial County, County of Santa Cruz, City of Watsonville
▼ Florida: Jackson County
▼ Georgia: Central Savannah River Area, Crisp Dooly
▼ Kentucky: Scott/McCreary Area
▼ Louisiana: Macon ridge, Northeast Louisiana Delta
▼ Michigan: Lake County
▼ Mississippi: North Delta
▼ Missouri: City of East Prairie, Mississippi County
▼ New Mexico: Mora, Rio Arriba and Taos County
▼ North Carolina: Halifax, Edgecombe, Robeson County, Wilson
▼ Ohio: Greater Portsmouth
▼ Southeast Oklahoma
▼ Oregon: Josephine County
▼ Pennsylvania: City of Lock Haven (Federal)
▼ South Carolina: Williamsburg-Lake City
▼ South Dakota: Beadle/Spink Dakota
▼ Tennessee: Scott/McCreary Area, Fayette County/ Haywood County
▼ Virginia: Accomack-Northampton
▼ Washington: Lower Yakima County
▼ West Virginia: Central Appalachia, McDowell County

Appendix B
African-American
Business Organizations

If you should need help in determining your specific needs. There are many African-American Business Organizations to help you on your journey to success. Here are a few:

Alpha Phi Chi Sorority
PO Box 1337
Florence AL 35630
205-764-4899

Professional Women in
Business Networking Systems
20220 S. Avalon Ave. #188
Carson CA 90746
310-542-7381

National Black Chambers of Commerce
5741 Tele graph Ave.
Oakland CA 94609
510-601-5741

U.S. African-American
Chamber of Commerce
117 Broadway
Jack London Waterfront
Oakland CA 94697
510-444-5741/510-510-5866 fax

American League of Financial
Institutions
1709 New York Ave. NW #801
Washington DC 20006
202-62 -5624

Blacks in Government
1820 11th St. NW
Washington DC 20001
202-66 -3280

Iota Phi Lambda Sorority, Inc
PO Box 11509
Montgomery AL 36111
205-984-0203

Association of Black
Women Entrepreneurs
PO Box 49363
Los Angeles CA 90049
213-624 -8639
Oakland Five East Bay Counties
Black Chamber of Commerce

117 Broadway
Oakland CA S4607
510-444-5741
Contact: Richard L. Meline

African-American Coalition
1100 6th St. SW
Washington DC 20024
202-488-7830

Association of Black
Foundation Executives
1828 L St. NW #300
Washington DC 20036
202-46 -6512

Conference of Minority Public
Administrators
1120 G St. NW #700
Washington DC 20005
202-393-7878
www.compa.org

Congressional Black Caucus House
Annex II-Ford Bldg - #344
Washington DC 20515
202-22 -7790

Executive Leadership Council
444 North Capitol St #715
Washington DC 20001
202-78 -6339

Lamda Kappa Mu Sorority, Inc.
1521 Crittendon St. NW
Washington DC 20011 202-82 -2368

Minority Business Enterprise Legal
Defense & Education Fund
2201 I St. #280
Washington DC 20002
202-51 -0010

National Urban Coalition
1875 Connecticut Ave. NW #400
Washington DC 20008
202-986-1460/202-986-1468 fax

National Political Congress of Black
Women, Inc.
600 New Hampshire Ave. NW #1125
Washington DC 20037
202-338-0800

Delta Sigma Theta Sorority , Inc
1707 New Hampshire ave. NW
Washington D 20009
202-986-2400

Institute for American Business
1511 "K" St. NW #438
Washington DC 20005
202-408-5418

Links Inc.
1200 Massachusetts Ave. NW
Washington DC 20005
202-842-8686

National Association of Negro Business &
Professional Women
1806 New Hampshire Ave. NW
Washington DC 20009
202-483 -4206
www.nanbpwc or
Contact: Clo Ivory, Exec. Dir.

National Black Leadership Roundtable
2135 Rayburn House Office Bldg
Washington DC 20515
202-331-2030

National Business League
1511 "K" St. NW #432
Washington DC 20005
202-737-4430/202-737-4432 fax

National Center for Neighborhood
Enterprise
136 Connecticut Ave. NW
Washington DC 20036
202-33 -1103

National Council for Equal Business
Opportunity
7932 West Branch Drive
Washington DC 20012
202-723 -8348

National Association of Minority
Contractors
666 11th St. NW #520
Washington DC 20001
202-347-8259
www.namc.org Contact: Arthor Queen

Phi Beta Sigma Fraternity, Inc.
145 Kennedy St. NW
Washington DC 20011
202-726 -5434/202-882-1681fax

Zeta Phi Beta Sorority, Inc.
1734 New Hampshire Ave NW
Washington DC 20009
202-387-3103

Black Women in Church & Societ Inter-
Denominational Theology Ctr
671 Beckwith St SW
Atlanta GA 30314
404-527-7740

National Council of Negro Women, Inc.
1627 "K" St. NW #700
Washington DC 20006
202-659-0006

National Association of Investment
Companies
733 15th St NW #700
Washington DC 20005
202-289-4336
www.naLichq.org
Contact: Bettye Lynn Smith

Omega Psi Phi Fraternity
271 Georgia Ave. NW
Washington DC 20001
202-667-7158

Thurgood Marshall Scholarship Fund
One Dupont Circle #710
Washington DC 20036
202-778-0818

100 Black Men of America, Inc.
127 Peachtree St NE #704
Atlanta GA 30303
404-525-7111

Jack & Jill of America, Inc
4761 Sylvan Drive
Savannah GA 31405
912-356-2194 / 912-352-1814 fax

Alpha Kappa Alpha Sorority
5656 S. Stony Island Ave.
Chicago IL 60637
312-684-1282

Operation PUSH (People United to Serve Humanity)
930 East 50th St.
Chicago IL 60615
312-373-3366
www.rainbowpush.org
Contact: Shamova Ward
Sward@rainbowpush.org

Sigma Gamma Rho Sorority, Inc.
8800 S. Stony Island Ave.
Chicago IL 60617
312-873-9000

National Association of African American Entrepreneurs
PO Box 1191
Indianapolis IN 46206
317-841-3717
Contact: Linda Clemons

Iota Phi Theta Fraternity, Inc
PO Box 7628
Baltimore MD 21207
301-792-2192

National Association for the Advancement of Colored People
4805 Mt Hope Drive
Baltimore MD 21215
410-358-8900
www.naacp.org
Contact: John White

National Black MBA Association, Inc.
180 North Michigan #1515
Chicago o IL 60601
312-296-2622

Phi Delta Kappa Inc.
8233 South M.L. King Drive
Chicago IL 60619
312-793-7379

United American Progress Assoc.
701 East 79th St.
Chicago IL 60619
312-955-8112

Alpha Phi Alpha Fraternity, Inc
231 Saint Paul St.
Baltimore MD 21218
410-554-0040

National Black Women's Consciousness-Raising Asso
1906 North Charles St.
Baltimore MD 21218
410-727-8900
anulane@aol.com
Contact: Elaine Simon

National Student Business League
7226 East Firest Road
Kentland MD 20785
202-895-3926

Brenda Alford
Alliance of Minority Women for Business & Political Development
PO Box 13933
Silver Spring MD 20911
301-565-0258

National Association of Urban Bankers
1010 Wayne Ave. #1210
Silver Spring MD 20910
301-589-2141

International Association of African &
Black Business People
18900 Schoolcraft St.
Detroit MI 48223

National Black United Fund, Inc.
50 Park Place #1538
Newark NJ 07102
201-643-5122

Caribbean Action Lobby
391 Eastern Parkway
Brooklyn NY 11216
718-773-8351
Contact: Waldaba Stewart

National Alliance of Black SalesMen and
SalesWomen
PO Box 2814-Manhattanville
Harlem NY 10027
718-409-4925

American Association of Black Women
Entrepreneurs
PO Box 13933
Silver Spring MD 20911
301-565-0258

Eta Phi Beta Sorority
16815 James Couzens
Detroit MI 48235
313-862-0060

National Association of Minority Women
in Business
906 Grand Ave. #1010
Kansas City MO 64106
816-421-3335

Zeta Delta Phi Sorority, Inc.
P.O. Box 157
Bronx NY 10469

Caribbean-American Chamber of
Commerce and Industry, Inc.
Brooklyn Navy Yard, Bldg #5
Brooklyn NY 11205
718-834-4544

Association of Minority Enterprises of
NY
250 Fulton Ave #505
Hempstead NY 11550
516-489-0120

African Business Association
271 Madison Ave #908
New York NY 10016
212-576-1219

Black Retail Action Group
PO Box 1192-Rockefeller Ctr Sta
New York NY 10185
212-308-6017

Interracial Council for Business
Opportunity
51 Madison Ave #2212
New York NY 10010
212-779-4360

National Urban League, Inc.
500 East 62nd St
New York NY 10021
212-310-9000

National Minority Supplier Development
Council Inc. '
15 West 39th St. - 9th Floor
New York NY 10018
212-944-2430

Sigma Pi Phi Fraternity
920 Broadway - #703
New York NY 10010
212-477-5550

Black Executive Exchange Program
c/o National Urban League
50 East 62nd St.
New York NY 10021

Interracial Council for Business Opportunity
51 Madison Ave. #2212
New York NY 10010
212-779-4360

National Coalition of 100 Black Women
38 West 32nd St. #1610
New York NY 10001
212-947-2196
www.ncbw.org
Contact: Douglas Arnold
Shirley Poole, Executive Director

National Minority Business Council
235 East 42nd St.
New York NY 10017
212-573-2385
www.nmbc.org
Contact: Julie Rodriguez

National Action Network
1941 Madison Avenue
New York NY 10035
212-987-5020
Contact: Reverend Al Sharpton
www.na.netemailhojl941@aol.com

Twenty-First Century Foundation
100 East 85th St.
New York NY 10028
212-249-3612

Third System
10 Saratoga Court
Ridge NY 71961
516-218-2405
Contact: Ron Samuel

National Economic Association
Office of Vice Provost
Pennsylvania State University University
Park PA 16802
814-865-4700

United Negro College Fund Inc.
8260 Willow Oaks Corp. Dr. #10444
Fairfax VA 22031
703-205-3400

Kappa Alpha Psi Fraternity, Inc
2322-24 North Broad St.
Philadelphia PA 19132
215-228-7184

Council on Career Development for
Minorities
1341 W. Mockingbird Lane #412E
Dallas TX 7527
214-631-3677
ccdm35@aol.com

Black Women's Network, Inc.
8712 West Spokane St.
Milwaukee WI 53224
414-353-8925

Appendix C
Philanthropies and Foundations

Here you will find real people, with real money, set up and maintained by individuals – some long ago, some now—to make a difference for and with you. Wake up and Smell the Dollars! Make a Difference!

Anheuser Busch Charitable Trust
One Busch Place
St. Louis, MO 63118
314-577-2433
Contact: Linda Salava

Atlantic Richfield Company
ARCO Foundation
515 S. Flower St.
Los Angeles, CA 90071
213-486-3342
Contact: Russell Sagaguchi

Bank Boston Corporation
Mail Stop 01-28-04
P.O. Box 2016
Boston, MA 02146
617-434-2804
www.llnl.gov/fstc/bank-of-boston.html
Contact: Michelle Courton Bronson

Bank of America Foundation
101 North First Ave.
Phoenix, AZ 85003
602-594-2656
Contact: Jane Tracey

Bush Foundation for Family Literacy
1112 16th St. NW – Suite 340
Washington, DC 20036
202-955-6183
www.barbarabushfoundation.com
Contact: Benita Somerfield, Executive Director

Coca Cola Foundation
P.O. Drawer 1734
Atlanta, GA 30301
404-676-2568
Contact: Donald R. Greene, Foundation President

Eastman Kodak Company
343 State St.
Rochester, NY 14650
716-724-1980
www.kodak.com
Contact: Essie L. Calhoun, President,
Charitable Trust

Exxon Education Foundation
5959 Las Colinas Boulevard
Irving, TX 75039
972-444-1104
www.exxon.com
Contact: Edward F. Ahnert, Contributions
Manager / Foundation President

Firestone Croger S.J. Foundation
105 S. Brynmawr Ave.
Brynmawr, PA 19010
610-520-9490
Contact: Herbert T. McDevitt, Executive
Administrator

Ford Foundation
320 East 43rd St.
New York, NY 10017
212-573-5000
www.fordfoundation.org
Contact: Lynda Mullen

General Motors Foundation
MC482-111-134
3044 West Grand Boulevard
Detroit, MI 48202
313-556-2057
Contact: Jeffrey M. Krause, Director, GM
Global Philanthropy

Harris Bank Foundation
111 West Monroe Street
P.O. Box 755
Chicago, IL 60690
312-461-5834
Contact: Streibich Curtis, Community
Affairs (Chicago Only)

Hearst (William Randolph) Foundation,
Inc.
90 New Montgomery Street – Suite 1212
San Francisco, CA 94105
415-543-0450
Contact: Thomas Eastham, Vice
President

Hearst Foundation
888 Seventh Avenue – 27th Floor
New York, NY 10106
212-586-5404
www.fdncenter.org/grantmaker/hearst

Hershey Foods Corporation
100 Crystala Drive
Hershey, PA 17033
717-534-7880
Contact: Andrea Bowerman, Corporate
Contributions Manager

Hughes Electronics Corporation
Building CO1, MS C122
P.O. Box 80028
Los Angeles, CA 90080
Contact: Maria Zumbrun, Manager,
Philanthropy

Intel Foundation
5200 NE Elam Young Parkway
Hillsboro, OR 97124
503-696-8093
www.intel.com/intel/community
Contact: Alisa Hampton, Program Officer

Katzenberger Foundation, Inc.
C/O Muchnick, Golieb & Golieb
630 Fifth Avenue - #1425
New York, NY 10111
212-315-5575
Contact: Abner J. Golieb, President

Kellogg (W.K.) Foundation
One Michigan Avenue East
Battle Creek, MI 49017
616-968-1611
www.wkkf.org

K-Mart Family Foundation
C/O K Mart Corporate Affairs
3100 West Big Beaver Road
Troy, MI 48084
248-643-5009
www.kmart.com
Contact: Wendy Kemp, Community Affairs

MCI Foundation
0617/001
1801 Pennsylvania Avenue, NW
Washington, DC 20006
202-887-3247
Charles Sweeney, Foundation Director

McDonalds Foundation Corporation
McDonalds Plaza
Oakbrook, IL 60521
630-623-7048
Contact: Ken Barun

Mobil Foundation
3325 Gallows Road
Fairfax, VA 22037
703-846-3381
www.mobil.com
Contact: Richard G. Mund, Foundation
Director

Poverty and Race Research Action
Council
1711 Connecticut Avenue NW – Suite 207
Washington, DC 20009
Contact: Chester Hartman, Executive
Director

Proctor & Gamble Company
P.O. Box 599 Cincinnati, OH 45201
513-983-1100 / 513-945-8454 Fax
www.pg.com/community
Contact: Carol G. Talbot, Contributions
and Community Relations
Brenda Ratliff

Public Welfare Foundation, Inc.
2600 Virginia Avenue NW, Room 505
Washington, DC 20037
202-965-1800
www.publicwelfare.org
Contact: Martha Bentley, Grants Manager

RJR Nabisco Foundation
1301 Avenue of Americas
New York, NY 10019
212-258-5600
Contact: Linda T. Elkes, executive
Director

Rockefeller Family Fund
437 Madison avenue – 37th Floor
New York, NY 10022
212-812-4252
www.rffund.org
Contact: Lee Wasserman, Director

Rockefeller Foundation
420 Fifth Ave.
New York, NY 10018
212-869-8500
Contact: Lynda Mullen

Schwab (Charles) Corporation Foundation
101 Montgomery Street – 26th Floor
San Francisco, CA 94104
415-636-7599
Contact: Cecilia McDonnell, Manager,
Community Affairs

Target Stores
P.O. Box 1392
Minneapolis, MN 55440
612-304-6073
Contact: Jeff Appelquist, Manager, Community Relations

TOSCO Marketing Company (Circle K Stores)
P.O. Box 52804
Phoenix, AZ 85072
602-728-4516
Contact: Julie Igo, Public Relations Manager

Wal-Mart Foundation
702 SW Eighth Street
Bentonville, AR 72716
501-273-4000
Contact: Emerson Goodwin, Foundation Director

Appendix D
Small Business Administration

Nationwide Offices and Information Centers

If you need advice, information or capital for your small business, call the SBA in your area.

Anchorage District Office
Box 67
122 W 8th Ave #A36
Anchorage AK 99513
907-271-4022/907-271-4545 fax

Little Rock District Office
2120 Riverfront Drive #100
Little Rock AR 72202
501-324-5871/501-324-5199 fax

Fresno District Office
2719 N. Air Fresno Drive #200
Fresno CA 93727
209-487-5791/209-487-5636 fax

Sacramento District Office
660 J Street #215
Sacramento CA 95814
916-498-6410/916-498-6422 fax

San Francisco District Office
455 Market St - 6th Floor
San Francisco CA 94105
415-744-6820/415-744-6812 fax

Santa Ana District Office
200 W Santa Ana Blvd #700
Santa Ana CA 92701
714-550-7420/714-550-0191 fax

Denver Regional Office
Region VIII
721 19th St #400
Denver CO 80202
303-844-0500/303-844-0506 fax

Birmingham District Office
2121 8th Avenue N - #200
Birmingham AL 35203
205-731-1341/205-731-1404 fax

Phoenix District Office
2828 N Central Ave #800
Phoenix AZ 85004
602-640-2316/602-640-2360 fax

Los Angeles District Office
330 N. Brand Blvd #1200
Glendale CA 91203
818-552-3210/818-552-3260 fax

San Diego District Office
550 West "C" St #550
San Diego CA 92101
619-557-7520/619-557-5894 fax

San Francisco Regional Office - Region IX
435 Market St #2200
San Francisco CA 94105
415-744-2118/415-744-2119 fax

Denver District Office
721 19th St #426
Denver CO 80202
303-844-2607/303-844-6468 fax

Hartford District Office
330 Main St - 2nd Floor
Hartford CT 06106
860-240-4700/860-240-4659 fax

National Women's Business Counsel -
Washington Office Ctr
409 3rd Street - #5850
Washington DC 20416
202-205-3850/202-205-6825 fax

Office of Entrepreneurial Dev.
Washington Office Center
409 3rd Street SW - #6200
Washington DC 20416
202-205-6706/202-205-6903 fax

Office of Financial Assistance
Washington Office Center
409 3rd Street - #8300
Washington DC 20416
202-205-6490/202-205-7064 fax

Office of Small Business Dev Ctr
Washington Office Center
409 3rd Street - #4600
Washington DC 20416
202-205-6766/205-7727 fax

Office of Government Contracting
Washington Office Center
409 3rd Street SW - #8000
Washington DC 20416
202-205-6479/202-205-7652 fax

Office of Capital Access
Washington Office Center
409 3rd Street - #8200
Washington DC 20416
202-205-6657/202-205-7230 fax

Washington District Office
1110 Vermont Ave. NW Suite 900 -
P.O. Box 34500
Washington DC 20005
202-606-4000/202-606-4225 fax

National SCORE Office Washington Office
Center 409 3rd Street - #6800
Washington DC 20416
202-205-6762/202-205-7064 fax

Office of Business Initiatives
Washington Office Center
409 3rd Street SW - #6100
Washington DC 20416
202-205-6665/202-205-7416 fax

Office of Advocacy
Washington Office Center
409 3rd Street SW - #7800
Washington DC 20416
202-205-6533/202-205-6928 fax

Office of Minority Enterprise
Development Washington Office Ct
409 3rd Street SW - #8000
Washington DC 20416
202-205-6412/202-205-7652 fax

Office of the Administrator
Washington Office Center
409 3rd Street SW - #7000
Washington DC 20416
202-205-6605/202-205-6802 fax

Office of Women's Business ownership/
Washington Office 409 3rd Street - #4400
Washington DC 20416
202-205-6673/202-205-7287 fax
http://www.sba.gov/womeninbusine

Wilmington Branch Office
824 N. Market St.- #610
Wilmington DE 19801
302-573-6294/302-573-6060 fax

Jacksonville District Office 7825
Baymeadow Drive #100-B
Jacksonville FL 32256
904-443-1900/904-443-1980 fax

Atlanta Regional Office Region IV -
S. Tower #496
1720 Peachtree Road NW
Atlanta GA 30309
404-347-4999/404-347-2355 fax

Agna Branch Office
First Hawaiian Bank Building
Suite 302 -400 Route 8
Mongmong GU 96927
671-472-7419/671-472-7365 fax

Cedar Rapids District Office
The Latner Building
215 4th Ave SE - #200
Cedar Rapids IA 52401
319-362-6405/319-362-7861 fax

Boise District Office 1020 Main St #290
Boise ID 83702
208-334-1696/208-334-9353 fax

Springfield Branch Office
511 West Capital Ave. #302
Springfield IL 62704
217-492-4416/217-492-4867 fax

Wichita District Office
100 East English St #510
Wichita KS 67202
316-269-6616/316-269-6499 fax

Miami District Office
100 S. Biscayne Blvd. 7th Floor
Miami FL 33131
305-536-5521/305-536-5058 fax

Atlanta District Office
1720 Peachtree Rd NW - 6th Floor
Atlanta GA 30309
404-347-4147/404-347-4745 fax

Honolulu District Office
Room 2-235, PO Box 50207
Honolulu HI 96850
808-541-2990/808-541-2976 fax

Des Moines District Office
210 Walnut St #749
Des Moines IA 50309
515-284-4422/515-284-4572 fax

Chicago Regional Office
Region V - Citicorp Center
500 West Madison St #1250
Chicago IL 60661
312-353-4528/312-886-5688 fax

Indianapolis District Office
429 N Pennsylvania St #100
Indianapolis IN 46204
317-226-7272/317-226-7529 fax

New Orleans District Office
365 Canal St #2550
New Orleans LA 70130
504-589-6685/504-589-2339 fax

Boston Regional Office
Region I - O'Neil Federal Bldg
10 Causeway St - #812
Boston MA 02222
617-565-8415/617-565-8420 fax

Baltimore District Office
City Crescent Building
10 South Howard St - #6220
Baltimore MD 21201
410-962-4392/410-962-1805 fax

Marquette Branch Office
501 South Front St.
Marquette MI 49855
906-225-1108/906-225-1109 fax

Kansas City Regional Office
Region VII - Lucas Place
323 West Eighth St #307
Kansas city MO, 64105
816-374-6380/816-374-6339 fax

Springfield Branch Office
620 South Glenstone St #110
Springfield MO 65802
417-864-7670/417-864-4108 fax

Gulfport Branch Office
2909 13th St #203
Gulfport MS 39501
228-863-4449/228-864-0179 fax

Helena District Office Federal Building
301 South Park - #344
Helena MT 59626
406-441-1081/406-441-1090 fax

Springfield Branch Office Suite 410
1441 Main Street
Springfield MA 01103
413-785-0268/413-785-0267 fax

Detroit District Office
477 Michigan Ave #515
Detroit MI 48226
313-226-6075/313-226-4769 fax

Minneapolis District Office
100 North 6th St #610
Minneapolis MN 55403
612-370-2324/612-370-2332 fax

Kansas City District Office
Lucas Place
323 West Eighth St #501
Kansas City MO 64105
816-374-6708/816-374-6759 fax

St. Louis District Office
815 Olive St #242
St. Louis MO 63101
314-539-6600/314-539-3785 fax

Jackson District Office
101 West Capital St #400
Jackson MS 39201
601-965-4378/601-965-5629 fax

Charlotte District Office
200 North College St #A2015
Charlotte NC 29401
803-853-3900/803-853-2529 fax

Fargo District Office
PO Box 3086
657 2nd Ave North #219
Fargo ND 58108
701-239-5131/701-239-5645 fax

New Jersey District Office
Two Gateway Center - 4th Floor
Newark NJ 07102
973-645-2434/973-645-6265 fax

Nevada District Office
300 Las Vegas Blvd S. #1100
Las Vegas NV 89101
702-388-6611/702-388-6469 fax

Elmira Branch Office
333 East Water St. - 4th Floor
Elmira NY 14901
607-734-8130/607-733-4656 fax

New York District Office
26 Federal Plaza - #31-00
New York NY 10278
212-264-4354/212-264-4963 fax

Rochester Branch Office
100 State Street - #410
Rochester NY 14614
716-263-7600/716-263-3146 fax

Cleveland District Office
1111 Superior Ave #630
Cleveland OH 44114
216-522-4180/216-522-2038 fax

Omaha District Office 11145 Mill Valley
Road Omaha NE 68154
402-221-4691/402-498-3611 fax

Albuquerque District Office
625 Silver Ave SW #320
Albuquerque NM 87102
505-346-7909/505-346-6711 fax

Buffalo District Office
111 West Huron Street - #1311
Buffalo NY 14202
716-551-4301/716-551-4418 fax

Melville Branch Office
35 Pinelawn Road - #207W
Melville NY 11747
516-454-0750/516-454-0769 fax

New York Regional Office
Region II
26 Federal Plaza - #3108
New York NY 10278
212-264-1450/212-264-0038

Syracuse District Office
401 South Salina St - 5th Floor
Syracuse NY 13202
315-471-9393/315-471-9288

Columbus District Office
2 Nationwide Plaza #1400
Columbus OH 43215
614-469-6860/614-469-2391 fax

Oklahoma City District Office
210 Park Ave #1300
Oklahoma City OK 73102
405-231-5521/405-231-4876 fax

Portland District Office
1515 SW Fifth Ave #1050
Portland OR 97201
503-326-2682/503-326-2808 fax

Philadelphia Regional Office
Region III - Rbt Nix Fed Bldg
900 Market Street - 5th Floor
Philadelphia PA 19107
215-580-2SBA/215-580-2800 fax

Providence District Office
5th Floor
380 Westminster Mall
Providence RI 02903
401-528-4561/401-528-4539 fax

Sioux Falls District Office
110 South Phillips Ave #200
Sioux Falls SD 57104
605-330-4243/605-330-4215 fax

El Paso District Office
10737 Gateway West #320
El Paso TX 79935
915-540-5586/915-633-7005 fax

Dallas/Ft Worth District Office
4300 Amon Carter Blvd #114
Fort Worth TX 76155
817-885-6500/817-885-6516 fax

Portland District Office
1515 SW Fifth Ave #1050
Portland OR 97201
503-326-2682/503-326-2808 fax

Philadelphia District Office
Robert NC Nix, Sr. Fed. Bldg
900 Market St. - 5th Floor
Philadelphia PA 19107
215-580-2SBA/215-580-2762 fax

Pittsburg District Office Federal Building
1000 Liberty Ave - Room 1128
Pittsburg PA 15222
412-395-6560/412-395-6562 fax

Columbia District Office
1835 Assembly St #358
Columbia SC 29201
803-765-5377/803-765-5962 fax

Corpus Christi Branch Office
606 N. Carancahua - #1200
Corpus Christi TX 78476
512-888-3331/512-888-3418 fax

Dallas Regional Office Region VI
4300 Amon Carter Blvd #108
Fort Worth TX 76155
817-885-6581/817-885-6588 fax

Houston District Office
9301 Southwest Freeway #550
Houston TX 77074

713-773-6500/713-773-6550 fax
Lubbock District Office
1205 Texas Ave. #408
Lubbock TX 79401
806-472-7462/806-472-7487 fax

Salt Lake City District Office
125 South State St #2229
Salt Lake City UT 84138
801-524-5804/801-524-4160 fax

Montpelier District Office
87 State St - #205, PO Box 605
Montpelier VT 05602
802-828-4422/802-828-4485 fax

Seattle Regional Office
Region X - Park Place Building
1200 Sixth Ave #1805
Seattle WA 98101
206-553-5676/206-553-4155 fax

Madison District Office
212 East Washington Ave #213
Madison WI 53703
608-264-5261/608-264-5541 fax

West Virginia District Office
Federal Center, Suite 330
320 West Pike Street
Clarksburg WV 26301
304-623-5631/304-623-0023 fax

San Antonio District Office
727 East Durango Blvd #A-527
San Antonio TX 78206
210-472-5900/210-472-5936 fax

Richmond District Office
Dale Building
1504 Santa Rosa Park - #200
Richmond VA 23229
804-771-2400/804-771-8018 fax

Seattle District Office
Park Place Building
1200 Sixth Avenue #1700
Seattle WA 98101
206-553-7310/206-553-7099 fax

Spokane District Office
801 West Riverside Ave #200
Spokane WA 99201
509-353-2809/509-353-2829 fax

Milwaukee Branch Office
310 W Wisconsin Ave. #400
Milwaukee WI 53203
414-297-3941/414-297-1377 fax

Casper District Office
PO Box 2839
100 East B St #4001
Casper WY 82602
307-261-6500/307-261-6535 fax

Appendix E
Beginning Exercise For Self Economic Empowerment

Make a Decision to Control Your Life...

Stop the act of blame and become totally responsible for self.

NOW!

Do you wish to have others make all decisions about your future?

If your answer is no, then start the process of empowering yourself by saying "I am responsible for my freedom from now on. I will take charge of my own emancipation through education."

Where I spend my money is to whom I give my power...

I pay rent ❑
I own my home ❑
I work for a company ❑
I own my own business ❑
I pay myself a salary ❑
I own shares in the company I work for ❑
I own stock in companies that are necessary to service modern life ❑

Electric Company	❑	Telephone Company	❑
Gas Company	❑	Water Company	❑
Food Chain	❑	Furniture Chain	❑
Insurance Company	❑	Clothing Company	❑
Bank	❑	Credit Union	❑
High Tech Communications Company			❑

I do not own stock in anything ❑
Do I know what stock my pension fund is supporting? Yes ❑ No ❑

How much of my money is invested in building the prison that houses over 4 million African-American and Latino males in our states? _____

How long have I known that slavery is legal in prisons? _____

How many of my family members and friends' family members am I supporting to remain in slavery with a payroll of 6 cents per hour? _____

How often do I contribute to the abuses of my own freedom? _____

When will enough be enough? _____

TODAY! ENOUGH IS ENOUGH!

I am ready for Self Economic Empowerment!